SPORTS IN THE LIVES OF CHILDREN AND ADOLESCENTS

Success on the Field and in Life

ROBERT S. GRIFFIN

Westport, Connecticut
London

Library of Congress Cataloging-in-Publication Data

Griffin, Robert S.
    Sports in the lives of children and adolescents : success on the
field and in life / Robert S. Griffin.
       p.   cm.
    Includes bibliographical references and index.
    ISBN 0–275–96127–3 (alk. paper)
    1. Sports for children—Psychological aspects. 2. Sports for
children—Social aspects. 3. Character. I. Title.
GV709.2.G75   1998
796′.083—DC21   97–33711

British Library Cataloguing in Publication Data is available.

Library of Congress Catalog Card Number: 97–33711
ISBN: 0–275–96127–3

First published in 1998

Praeger Publishers, 88 Post Road West, Westport, CT 06881
An imprint of Greenwood Publishing Group, Inc.

Printed in the United States of America

The paper used in this book complies with the
Permanent Paper Standard issued by the National
Information Standards Organization (Z39.48–1984).

10 9 8 7 6 5 4 3 2

To Ken Heise

Contents

Acknowledgments

Many people contributed to this book, some a long time ago and some without realizing it, I'm sure. Seven people I want to thank publicly for being especially helpful: Professor Nancy Wessinger, who was generous with her time, advice, and materials when I was initially exploring the research in the area of sports and children. My agent, Diane Cleaver (sadly, Diane died recently), who "got" the book—that it is about more than just sports, and that what it is about, including sports, is important. Her encouragement was invaluable when others were saying, "Why are you giving all that energy to a book about kids' sports?" Ted Knight, who contributed greatly to the book's organization and syntax. Lynn Taylor and Norine Mudrick at Praeger, who were so supportive. Salli Griggs, who provided superb secretarial assistance. And last, Li Xia: the example she sets in the way she lives her life and her relationship with me inspired me to do my absolute best with this project.

CHAPTER 1

Introduction

I remember when I opened Ken Heise's letter. It was a pleasant, sunny morning in late August, over a year ago as I write this. I was in my office at the University of Vermont, where I am on the faculty in education. I was going through a pile of mail that had accumulated over the summer while I had been in Finland doing some lecturing and consulting. The school year would begin in a few days.

In addition to taking care of correspondence that had been stacked neatly on my desk, the day was to be dedicated to getting back into the swing of things at the university, preparing courses I would be teaching in the upcoming semester, checking on committee assignments, and seeing what colleagues on the faculty had been up to. After about five minutes of going through university memoranda, notices of professional meetings, and advertisements for text materials, I found that this undertaking was getting tedious. I decided it might brighten my day if instead of taking mail from off the top of the pile, I would sort down through the stack and find some "real" letters—that is, with envelopes you buy at the drug store, written by hand, and affixed with a stamp you have to lick to get to stick in place.

The first real letter I found had been postmarked in Collierville, Tennessee three weeks earlier. The return address said it was from a Ken Heise—no one I knew. "Wonder what this is about," I thought, as I opened the envelope and read the single hand-written sheet of paper:

Dear Professor Griffin:

My wife and I disagree on whether our children should participate in school athletics. My daughter is 10 and my son is 6. My daughter is interested in basketball and my son likes all sports. Personally, I played basketball and ran track in high school and took judo in college. My wife says sports are a waste of time, that there is the risk of injury and they detract from social development and schoolwork. But I—and other men I know agree with me—see sports as building character and developing a work ethic. While my daughter gets excellent grades in school, she seems to be bored much of the time, and I think sports would help. When I told my wife of how I look at it, she wasn't convinced. "Prove it to me!" she said. I spent a whole day at the library, but all I could find was two references to your article on the McAteer PASS project. Although your article put school sports in a good light, it didn't come close to satisfying my wife—she is still highly skeptical about the value of athletics. I am not sure where to go with this. Since yours is the only thing I could find, I thought I'd write and see if you could refer me to any studies or follow-up investigations on sports and later success in life. I just don't know what journals might have research of this kind. Can you be of assistance? If you do get back to me on this, I will refer your answer to *The Commercial Appeal*, the local Memphis newspaper, because I know other people could benefit from this information.

Thanks for any assistance you can provide.

Sincerely,
Ken Heise

The article of mine that Ken referred to is about a program operating successfully in several high schools that helps student-athletes perform better academically. For some time I have had a professional interest in exploring sport psychology and coaching strategies with reference to how they shed light on what is happening in schools and to find approaches employed in athletics that can be applied in the classroom.[1] As a part of that concern, in the mid-1980s I set up a summer course at the University of Vermont called "Promoting Achievement in Sport and School" to foster an exchange among sports professionals and educators who have other frames of reference. The instructor of that course, sport psychologist Dr. Joel Kirsch, discussed with me his idea for an elective high school class that would encourage athletes to apply in the classroom the concepts, values, and skills that support their success on the field. He and his wife, educator Susan Kirsch, have developed such a course ("Promoting Achievement in School through Sports"—PASS), and I have stayed in touch with its progress. Impressed with what I have observed, I decided to publish a piece on it, the one that Ken read.[2]

Ken's letter intrigued me, and a week later I started to write him a response. I assumed a brief letter would do, perhaps a page or two. Basically I saw myself responding to his request for advice on how to move forward in his own investigations, something he could submit to the Memphis newspaper. However, as I started to write I found myself thinking about the discussion he and his wife were having and wanting to respond to that. "Well, what about it?" I thought. "Does sports develop character? Does athletics contribute to the development of a good work ethic? Or, as Ken's wife contends, does it get in the way of a child's schoolwork and inhibit social development? What do I think about that? What do I *know* about that? Just what *are* the consequences of youngsters' involvement in sports? Is it a good thing or a bad thing?" As a professional educator, and given the work I had already been doing, I especially wanted to address the effects of a student's participation in school athletic programs.

While I was writing to Ken, images from my own childhood kept popping up. As a youngster I had been immersed in sports. I have pictures of myself in a baseball uniform at age 6. Sports was embedded in my sense of who I was, what I could and should be, and my relationships with, well, with everything in my life, including my family, especially my dad, and friends and school. My professional concern with sports had focused on the insights and practices I could derive from that domain that could be applied to improving schools. Writing this letter brought to the surface different, larger issues related to the role of sports in children's lives, and in my own life. What impact, for good or bad, does sports have on growing up in America and on the adults we become?

As the pages piled up—to my surprise, I wrote for at least two hours—it struck me how little I was actually sure about in all of this. Does sports really develop good character? In truth I hadn't seriously investigated that question or thought it through. Does participation in athletics enhance academic achievement or hinder it? If it can cut both ways, when or who does it help and when or who does it hurt? In spite of all my years as a serious athlete and all the time I've spent around sports and athletes, in spite of all my work in education as a high school teacher and university professor, I wasn't at all sure. And the fact that Ken had both a daughter and a son raised another question: What about girls in athletics? What is going on there? What could it be? What should it be? And then there were those studies Ken asked about, the ones that examine whether sports contributes to success later in life: although it seemed certain that research had focused on this concern, I wasn't familiar with it. Ken had been unable to locate this kind of research or find answers to his other questions in his library search, and since I have had a good deal of practice locating research results, I thought I could probably be of help to him in this regard.

Even though Ken hadn't asked for it, I wanted to give him advice: I wanted to say either "Yes, you should encourage your children in organized sports" or "No, you shouldn't." But a firm—and most important, an informed—position was not there. This surprised me; until this moment I had been confident that sports was one area about which I was informed and resolved.

After two hours or so of writing, I had scrawled about ten yellow legal pages of ruminations, speculations, associations, questions, and guesses. Looking it over, it seemed too incoherent for anyone to make sense of—clearly unmailable. "Let it sit for a week or two," I told myself. "Get on with other things and let this whole business bounce around in your head, and then take another crack at writing the letter." That sounded best, so I paperclipped Ken's letter to my musings and placed the pages on a shelf just above my desk, right about eye level, in plain sight.

As time went by, events kept reminding me of Ken's letter and my aborted reply. The morning after I tried to answer Ken's letter, the local newspaper carried a wire story containing a list of the people children most admire, and there, among the president and movie stars and musicians and Mom and Dad, were several professional athletes. A few days after that, a half-page in the Sunday sports section was devoted to the issue of whether athletes ought to serve as role models for youth. Bo Jackson—former baseball and football star in both college and the pros—contended that they shouldn't. He asserted that being a role model was the obligation of parents, not athletes. In contrast, baseball slugger Juan Gonzales argued just as strongly for the opposite view, that sports stars should welcome the responsibility of being a positive example for youth. Reading along, I thought to myself that whatever one may think is preferable, the fact is that athletes *are* role models for many youngsters and that the question then becomes what the lives of sports heroes exemplify—what values, what standards, what priorities—and what difference that makes to children's lives and to our society.

I spend a great deal of my time observing in schools. The following week in a sixth grade health class I was visiting, the teacher asked her students to draw a picture of themselves that showed who they are, depicted them doing something they are proud of, or illustrated something they like to do. It was early in the school year, and the assignment was an introduce-yourself-to-others activity. Even though the assignment conceptually seemed a little cloudy to me, the students—twenty or so 12-year-old suburban kids, evenly divided between boys and girls—seemed to catch on right away and got right to the task, heads bent over, markers flying.

When it came time to hold up their drawings and explain them to the class, some children needed a bit of coaxing, but most all of them got it done. After the first four or five presentations, I realized that a pattern was forming: most of their pictures were about sports, and this was true of the girls as much as the boys. The pictures didn't all have to do with organized sports; a few showed activities such as playing touch football with friends, swimming, hunting, or fishing. I didn't get an exact count, but the preponderance of sports-oriented pictures involved the "major" sports of baseball, football, basketball, hockey, and soccer. I found it quite remarkable that sports are so pervasive in kids' lives; or, at least, how sports are what they bring up when they are asked to tell about themselves.

I couldn't help but notice as these children shared their drawings, how many of them were wearing the logos of professional and college athletic teams. With their hats, T-shirts, sweatshirts, jackets, and other sports paraphernalia, more than a few youngsters these days are walking advertisements for NBA, NFL, NHL, major league baseball, and college sport teams. It is what these children want to wear, and it is the image they wish to present to the world. Some of them reveal a totally sports-oriented self-presentation, from the tops of their heads down to the substantial Nikes or Reeboks on their feet—sneakers that through the magic of advertising have come to signify much more than a way to cushion and support one's feet.

At the time I visited this class, baseball-type hats—most of which were from athletic teams—were especially popular among the boys. Most classes in the school were dotted with hats. In one school near where I live, "wearing the hat" became a cause célèbre among the kids after the administration tried to ban the wearing of hats in school. The students got up in arms and conducted an organized protest, and the school leadership caved in—hats were back. From the kids' perspective, something important is clearly at stake with these sports hats.

The next week, in the same class that did the drawings, I was present when three high school students—two boys and a girl—were guest speakers. One of the boys and the girl were star basketball players, and the other boy was a high-scoring hockey player. The teacher introduced the three to the class as athletes. But this wasn't to be an hour just about sports, the teacher told her students. She wanted the session to deal primarily with adjusting to high school life and being a teenager, issues these sixth graders would soon face.

"Well," the teacher addressed the class, "what questions do you have for our guests?"

As it turned out, practically every question the younger students asked had to do with sports: "How old were you when you got started playing?" "What's the most fun thing about playing sports?" "Do you ever get nervous?" "Do you want to play in college?"

As the hour passed, I was struck by what nice young people the three student-athletes were. They came across as sincere, decent, hard-working, respectful, and balanced young adults (two were seniors and one a junior), and there was nothing the least bit arrogant about them. Their message was that sports in high school were great, but to be successful at them you had to work really hard—yet it was worth every bit of the time and effort. All three made it a point to mention the necessity of keeping up their grades and not slacking off in class.

Watching this exchange, I reflected on the interweaving of sports and schools and adolescence. It wasn't by chance, I decided, that these particular three students had been selected to give advice to those coming along behind them, and that they were identified as athletes. I also took note of the rather diffident, and mechanical, and rehearsed manner the three guest speakers had in common. It seemed to me that I had observed this personality type quite often among student-athletes. Was this personal style to any degree conditioned by the sports experience, or are people with this style drawn to sports? I wanted to think more about that.

Later in the afternoon I happened to be in the high school attended by the three student-athlete guest speakers. As I passed by the main office, I paused to look through the glass at the well-stocked trophy case, with its inscribed footballs and basketballs and so on. It was the biggest, most prominent feature in sight. "Sports certainly is a big deal in school," I thought to myself. "What's that all about?" Why are schools so deeply involved in the sports business? What are the consequences for the students and for the schools?

Some of the team pictures were getting a bit colored with age, and I was struck with how distant 1977 seemed. (Did we really think hair looked good like that?) I wondered what the kids in these old pictures are doing now and what effect playing high school sports had on their lives as adults. What impact will sports have on the three teenage presenters I had observed that morning in the sixth grade class?

A short time later, I met with a group of twelve high school seniors to talk about their college plans. The students didn't know each other, so I thought I'd try a get-acquainted activity. I asked each of them to tell us their name and to say something about themselves that would help us know them a bit better: an interest or hobby, something they had done lately, a movie or book they had liked, a place they had visited, or it could be an accomplishment or some personal characteristic—it was a very open-ended activity. As we went around the circle, it was the sixth grade drawings all over again. At least half the seniors (again, girls as well as boys) offered comments such as, "I really like to play field hockey and hope to play in college," "I'm a big Red Sox fan," "I am interested in basketball." Sports again. I found it striking.

Later, I was in the university library doing research for an article on education.[3] Being sensitized by this time to the sports topic, when I noticed that the table of contents of the educational journal I was reading contained two articles about sports, I decided to take the time to read them. I especially noticed a statement in the first article, "Let's Return Athletics to the Curriculum":

Among skills acquired and shaped by sports education are: learning teamwork; recognizing interdependence among teammates; attaining self-control; developing dependability; reaping the rewards of perseverance; appreciating the value of following rules; becoming skilled in thinking ahead; developing self-reliance; confidence building; experiencing individual and collective pride; participation in public presentations; valuing discipline; learning the virtues of practice and participation; learning how to win and lose gracefully; using sound judgment, developing a sense of strategy, and building and maintaining physical endurance, strength, stamina, grace, and agility.[4]

The second article, "Sports' Unsung Heroes," featured case studies of four exemplary adults and the ways their sports involvement when they were young shaped them into the adults they had became. It included the following passage:

The traits shared by our four unsung heroes are a high energy level, ability to focus energies, strong desire to achieve, positive attitude toward self and tasks to be accomplished, self-management skills, a balance between individual effort and teamwork and the ability to get to the root of the problem while those around them are dealing with the symptoms of a problem.[5]

The unstated premise, of course, was that sports accounted for these characteristics.

If you think about it—read back over them—these excerpts contain some very strong claims. I asked myself: "What other area in American life enjoys such a favorable image? Is any other activity considered to have such positive byproducts?" I suppose entering a religious order might be assumed to significantly develop a person; and the military—especially the Marines—is thought to hold out the possibility of enhancing those who undertake its regimen. But even so, I can't imagine either taking up a religious vocation or making a career of the military being credited with greater personal benefits than those attributed to participation in athletics.

The two sports articles I just quoted were published in an academic journal, so I looked for some documentation for the strong assertions about the skills- and traits-building qualities of sports participation. What sources, what research, did these authors cite to support their conclusions concerning the benefits of athletics? In his letter Ken

Heise had asked about studies linking sports to later success in life, and I thought I might list one or two from these articles when I finally wrote back to him. However, the authors had offered no documentation for their contentions. There were no footnotes or references to back up their assertions that participation in sports contributed to self-reliance, good judgment, the desire to achieve, problem-solving ability, and the rest. Nor was there any argumentation; there was no attempt to demonstrate to the reader how this happened. Instead, the assertion was just set out there: this is the result of playing sports, period.

My guess is that these authors were not consciously negligent or devious in failing to document the claims they were making for sports. I think they simply did not believe that their assertions needed verification. They never felt pressed to do more than *tell* the reader about the connection between sports and certain valued outcomes. I believe they were operating within what could be termed *cultural understandings* about sports, and that these understandings, these assumptions, provided the context for their writing. Indeed, although sport most certainly has detractors, overall it has enough favorable "spin" to free anyone who lauds it from having to provide much, if any, support for their assertions.

I don't think I am stretching it to say that a mythology has developed around sports. Myths serve to explain reality, give things meaning, and provide direction; they do not invite scrutiny and debate. Myths are reiterated (haven't we heard the claims offered in those excerpts before?), not questioned. Sitting in the library with these two articles before me, I realized that the mythology of sports needs probing, and that perhaps I should take it upon myself, even in some small measure, to do it.

On the way out of the library, I checked out four books on sports and quickly read them—I was getting hooked on the topic. One was *Sports Without Pressure* by psychologist Eric Margenau.[6] Margenau is unequivocal about the value of sports. He declares that "an early and frequent exposure to sports produces children who are healthier both physically and emotionally, and who grow up to become healthier adults."[7] He contends that sports gives children the opportunity to fantasize about being a hero and boosts their self-esteem by providing the chance to perform. Furthermore, Margenau notes, there is benefit to be gained from the personal identification derived from belonging to a group and being on a team. Moreover, there is the satisfaction of peer approval and the joy of trying to achieve something your friends are trying to achieve. Finally, sports offers a chance for the whole family to be involved in an activity, and it is a way for parents and children to establish better communications.[8]

"An athletic experience," Margenau writes, "is not only good, but *essential for all children*" [his emphasis]. He adds, "In my opinion, a parent who says that he or she is not interested in sports and doesn't value athletics for their children is acting irresponsibly."[9] This is putting it very forcefully to parents: encouraging your children in sports isn't a choice; it is an imperative. As a therapist with extensive experience in clinical settings, Margenau's views deserve serious consideration. He certainly raises the stakes in this entire business—from sports as simply a matter of fun and games, if you will, to something far more important. He directs parents to "Provide your child with a sports experience regardless of how you personally feel about the importance of sport."[10] That kind of statement gets your attention.

As with the two sports articles, I went "documentation hunting" in the Margenau book. When he made statements such as there being "considerable research on the subject and most of it supports the close connection between physical activity and mental health,"[11] I made it a point to see if I could find out precisely what research he had in mind, but again I came up empty. The result of my efforts wasn't so much that I doubted his veracity or competence. Instead, I concluded, as with the previous articles, that Margenau probably didn't feel he had to provide documentation. However, my experience did heighten my desire to seek out the relevant research and discover what it did say.

The second book I took from the library was *Dreams of Glory*, which turned out to be a delightful read. Written by the mother of a high school football player, it chronicles a season of her son's team.[12] Before that experience, the author, Judy Oppenheimer, admits she had viewed athletes as "fools, nonintellectuals, [and] macho jerks."[13] But what an effect that season had on her! She ended up

being insane about football. More than soccer, more than basketball, more than any sport I had ever come in contact with, I purely adored the entire wild, maddened, electric, power-pumping totality of the game. Football unleashed something primitive buried inside me, something that had always been there, waiting to spring to life. A coach would later tell me at length about the need to unearth the buried animal when training players, the animal that lies dormant in our soul. Well, football released my animal, too. Even that epiphany should have come as no surprise, really—I had known from the start that this game exerted a powerful pull on my heart.[14]

"Like it or not," Oppenheimer writes, "sport forms a man,"[15] and she wanted see how that process worked. After closely following her son's team from preseason practices to the last game of the year, she became convinced that the boys on that team learned some highly valuable lessons. In her words, they had learned something about "courage and hard work, about facing fears, about putting themselves on the line."[16] No one can deny that these are crucially important outcomes. There isn't a parent who doesn't care about these qualities, and wonder where and when—if ever—his or her child will come by them. If indeed sport can have this positive impact on children, it deserves our closest attention.

The third book I read was by Penelope Eckert, *Jocks and Burnouts: Social Categories and Identity in the High School.*[17] Eckert underscores (and we all know this from our own high school experience) that for many youngsters, sports is more than just what they do; in very large measure, sports is who they are. Sports for more than a few young people is a self-definition, as well as the concept that others have of them. Sports provides a way to think and behave. It provides a slot to occupy in the scheme of things, in school and beyond. Reading Eckert's book, I smiled to think about how prone teenagers are to type their schoolmates and themselves. In addition to *jocks*, a few of the labels for students over the past few years have included *normies, nerds, preppies, cowboys, skaters, wavers, rockers, stoners,* and *hardcores,* to mention but a few.[18] It isn't just students invested in sports that get put in a category, but still, I wonder if any label has greater influence on a person than *jock* or *athlete.* Eckert's descriptions made me want to explore what it means to see yourself—and to have others see you—as a jock.

The fourth book I took from the library was written in the 1970s and has become a classic in this area: James Michener's *Sports in America.*[19] It is clear that Michener loved sports, but at the same time he was distressed by a number of its tendencies, among them the trend toward an overemphasis on athletics in schools, excessive commercialization, violence, autocracy, the use of drugs, a win-at-any-cost competitive mentality, overzealous parents, and the phenomenon of sport-obsessed kids letting their academic opportunities slide away from them. Michener's analysis—and his ambivalence—about sports increased my desire to resolve some of my own reservations about sports.

It became increasingly clear that I wanted to spend time investigating the questions that Ken Heise's letter initially had raised, along with the issues that emerged from my subsequent research and reflection. Getting into this deeper, I thought, might satisfy the curiosity that had been growing in me. It might help clarify the significance of sports to my own life, as well as shed light on the impact of sports on the lives of children today—Ken's and others. It also might give direction to my future work involving sports. Perhaps, I thought, there are things I can learn and then communicate to other parents who have the same concerns as Ken and his wife. Perhaps even young athletes could get something out of what I had to say.

It was at this point that I finally answered Ken's letter:

Dear Ken:

I apologize for the long delay in getting back to you about your letter of last August, the one that asked me what I thought of your daughter and son's participation in sports. I actually didn't get it until late that month when I returned from some work in Europe, and then, well, I'll explain.

[I then recount what I have said here.]

I'm exploring the possibility of writing a book that essentially answers your letter. Your letter nicely frames the basic issues. It is significant that you are asking these questions about both your son and daughter. Of course there was a time, and not so very long ago, when this was only a concern with boys. I know that you and your wife are not alone with this issue of whether to encourage your children in sports. Sports plays such a big part in so many children's lives, and by and large parents are left with conventional wisdom and their own devices in responding to these realities. I'll see what I can learn from the literature (studies, argumentation, etc.) and let you know what I find out. I'll give you a call to learn more about you and your wife's discussions and your situation. Meanwhile, feel free to get in touch with me any time.

I did talk to Ken on the phone a week or so later. (His last name, Heise, is pronounced HIGH-see.) He began our conversation by telling me about a report he had seen on television of a study indicating that female athletes were less likely to smoke and do drugs, and that they made better grades in school. During our exchange, Ken emphasized that he has no doubt about the value of sports for his daughter and son. He thinks sports can help them become motivated to succeed and teach them how to win. Ken wants his children to be successful at what they do now and in the future, and to develop confidence in themselves. As he puts it, he wants them to have an "I can do it!" attitude. He views sports as crucial in the promotion of these qualities in his children.

His daughter, Julie, he informed me, is "my girl"—which I took to mean she is more aligned with or closer to Ken than to his wife, Melissa. Julie shoots baskets really well, Ken said, but she isn't interested in participating in sports or any other extracurricular activities, and he feels bad about that. As far as Ken can tell, Julie mostly sits around and listens to music and is bored much of the time. He is certain that sports would help break her inactivity and boredom.

When Julie was 5 years old, Ken recounted, he pretty much forced her to play sports even though she didn't want to. Recalling this brought up for Ken the question of whether a parent should insist that a child play sports, or partake in anything else the parent is convinced will be good for the child. On the one hand, parents don't want to compel children to do something against their will; it doesn't seem fair, and it could lead them to associate compulsion with the activity and turn them off to it when they might otherwise have enjoyed and profited from it. But then again, children don't always know what is best for them. It is likely that only later will they realize the worth of an undertaking, but by then it will be too late. Both Ken and I spoke of how we wished our parents had forced us to keep up with our music lessons when we were kids. However, the issue remained unresolved in our conversation, and I made a mental note that the question of parent insistence was something I needed to cover in the book I was beginning to plan.

Ken described his son David as quiet and somewhat of a "momma's boy," a lovable kid, a "hugger," as he put it. Although Ken didn't say so directly, I got the idea that he sees a need to masculinize his son, to break the overly close bond between David and his mother and somewhat defuse David's identification with her. As Ken spoke about David, I recalled a conversation I had had just the day before with a mother of an 11-year-old boy. She told me that she is a single parent and that her son's father isn't in his life very much. She wants to raise a—she groped for a way to put it—"well, I want to raise a man, a strong man, do you know what I mean?" I replied that I thought I did know what she meant. She wondered whether a sports experience might be good for her son. We talked about it for a few minutes, and it brought up for me the question of what gender means these days and what sports has to do with masculinity and femininity. There was another issue I needed to consider in the book.

Ken said that David wasn't very well coordinated, and that he had kept him out of tee-ball for fear that David might get hurt. Ken told me that David was the sort who was "interested in everything." He mentioned David's strong interest in math as an example. Ken said he expected David to be interested in sports as a spectator if not as a participant. Again the issue came up of how much a parent ought to encourage sports involvement. As convinced as Ken was of the worth of sports, should he push it hard with David? (I thought of Margenau's contention in *Sports Without Pressure* that it is vital that parents provide a sports experience for their child.) Or, Ken wondered, should he let events run their course with Julie and David? I was pretty sure this would be very difficult for Ken to do, given his beliefs about sports and his dedication as a father. For me, it came down to the validity of Margenau's argument: Was he right about the essential nature of sports in a child's life? I wanted to resolve that question for myself and write about it.

Ken and I spoke for perhaps forty-five minutes in all, and we agreed to keep in contact with one another. When I hung up the phone, I took out a note pad and tried to organize my thoughts. What, I asked myself, did I want from these explorations I was embarking upon?

The first thing I wrote down was that I wanted to become clearer about my own life. When I was growing up, sports (in my case, that meant the team sports of football, basketball, and baseball) were everything to me. Although my dad was older and not an active participant in sports when I knew him (he was 50 years old when I was born), he was an avid fan, especially of baseball. Among my most prominent memories are the two of us going to baseball games together. I realized early on that it would be a dream come true for my dad if I became a professional baseball player.

Dad was a barber in a hotel shop and many professional baseball players, both from our local minor league team and visiting players, were his customers. When I was about 10 years old, Dad told me one day that he had mentioned to one of the visiting players (from the Columbus Red Birds, a Saint Louis Cardinals farm team at that time) that I was very interested in baseball and on a team and quite a good player. The player said that he would like to meet me and that he would leave passes for the next game at the gate for Dad and me. He told Dad that I should come down to the field before the game began and say hello to him.

Dad and I took the bus to the game, picked up the passes (*passes*, we were somebody!), and got to our seats about halfway up on the third base side. Immediately Dad poked me and pointed and said, "There he is, Bobby, go down there and talk to him." The player—whose name I can't remember; I wonder if I ever knew it—in his red and gray visiting uniform was down on the field playing catch with a teammate. I was paralyzed. In those years I didn't talk to any adult very much, and certainly not to an adult who wasn't even a relative. And to a *ballplayer? Down on the field?* Earlier it had sounded great and I was excited. But now I was terrified.

"Get down there, Bobby, before he leaves. Go ahead, just walk right down there—he knows you're coming."

Somehow I made it down the steps and somehow the player knew it was me and walked over. I remember very little about our conversation. Mostly I remember how kind he was. He asked me what position I played, and I said the infield, shortstop and third base. He inquired about my batting average and I answered .600 (you have averages like that at ten in the peewee league I was playing in). I must have been a tough interview for him; I never looked up much at all. I don't know if I ever really saw his face. I do have a memory of his forearms, though, so muscular as they rested on the railing next to mine, and I remember the impressive leather glove—a real ballplayer's glove!—that engulfed his hand. If I could just grow up to be like him, wouldn't that be something! We finished our conversation, he wished me good luck in my ballplaying, and I walked back up to where Dad was sitting. I could see his smile as I approached. What a wonderful time it was on that sunny day, with my hot dog and Coke, sitting right next to my dad watching the game.

It turned out that I did have some talent for baseball, especially as a hitter, and although I played other sports, I mainly concentrated on baseball. The summer I graduated from high school, I played American Legion baseball and did extremely well. I had just turned 17 and had grown several inches that year and put on some needed weight. The ball started to carry, and I began to get attention from the pro scouts. I had the chance to play professionally, but I couldn't accept the offer because I had signed up in an Army Reserve program and was scheduled to leave for active duty that August. I continued to play baseball in the Army and then in college and in amateur leagues, but the pro offers never came again. I have always regretted missing the chance to play professional ball. Looking back, I can see that I wasn't good in enough phases of the game to have had a realistic chance of making the majors, or of even lasting in the minors. I suppose that I would have lasted a couple of months in some low minor league before being released. But I still wish I would have had the chance to give it a try. If nothing else, I would have had a lifetime's worth of memories. And Dad would have been so proud to tell his customers about me in the shop during the short time before cancer took him away from us.

Writing this book has been a way for me to clarify what sports has meant and continues to mean in my own life. However, my own story is only a small part of this book. Mostly what I have sought to do is confront the questions about sports and children that were raised by my contact with Ken Heise. I have the background, the resources, and the time to do what most parents don't have the opportunity to do. Perhaps through this effort I will be of some assistance to them.

I have concluded that in order to answer in the best way the very interesting and important questions Ken has posed about his children and sports, it is essential to answer some larger questions about sports; doing that will put sports in a broader perspective and provide a context for making sense of the more immediate issue of what to do with one's children. Most of the questions have already surfaced in these pages, and they are the ones I confront in the various chapters of this book:

- What impact does sports have on growing up: on self-image, relationships, and overall effectiveness as an individual?
- How does participation in sports affect academic success?
- What effect does sports have on personal character (responsibility, hard work, self-discipline, autonomy, and morality)?
- Is competition good or harmful?
- Why is sports so prominent in schools?
- Does sports keep kids in school and out of trouble?
- What about girls in sports?
- What about sports for low-income and minority youth?
- What are good athletes like and how do they get that way? (This information may give parents clues as to how to contribute to their children's success in sports.)
- How can parents best support their children with regard to sports?

This book offers my research and my best thinking on these questions. My focus in these pages is on organized athletics—youth leagues, school programs, and the like—rather than on informal or solo activities such as pick-up games in the neighborhood or hunting and fishing. The task I set for myself in this book is to help Ken Heise and other parents reach their own conclusions about their children and sports. I have tried to frame the issues related to organized sports and provide information and a point of view in a such way that it will be useful. I hope what I offer sheds light on how widely and deeply sports permeates our lives and our society. Although I love sports and it has been a big part of my life, I have no vested interest in promoting or selling sports as an endeavor. I write from the perspective of an educator who cares about the totality of a child's life. As far as I am concerned, if sports truly contributes to a child's happiness and well-being, fine; if it doesn't, then so be it.

In his letter Ken asked about studies, investigations, and journals that would shed light on the issues. I refer to and discuss a number of resources throughout the book. Note the sources at the back of the book. A good way to augment your reading of this book is to browse the sports and parenting sections of a large bookstore for works that address these concerns. Reference librarians can be very helpful in answering your questions and identifying resources. In particular, there are now a number of computer databases that librarians can show you how to use. Take note of newspaper stories and magazine articles. Feel free to interview anyone or to call or write to anyone. Phone or write to newspaper reporters or magazine authors. You can generally get in touch with authors through their publishers, and journal authors at their institution, which is usually a university. (Libraries will have addresses if they aren't in the original source.) Talk to coaches and athletes and others involved in sports. Discuss this topic with your own children. Talk to other parents—anyone you think might be helpful to you. Ask: What do you think? Who else should I talk to? What should I go see, or read?

I am not so presumptuous as to represent myself as the last word on this subject. Rather, I see myself as one more voice at the table. I invite you to bring all that you have experienced and all that you value and know to what I write. Consider this a conversation with me. Perhaps together you and I can make some progress with these concerns. If nothing else, I hope that what I have written will stimulate you to focus your attention a bit more closely on the nature and impact of what I am convinced is a very important aspect of our culture and the lives of our children.

CHAPTER 2

Sports and Growing Up

Last summer when I was in Minneapolis for a long weekend to see my brother Walter and his family, the Griffins set out for the park to play baseball. Packed into a van on this beautiful Saturday afternoon were my brother and I, my two nephews, 7-year-old Neil and 13-year-old Leif, and my niece, 14-year-old Erin. Along the way we picked up Brian, a friend of Leif's.

Riding along squished into the middle of the front seat holding a borrowed glove and bat, I had the secure and contented feeling that I associate with sports. I remember on Saturdays when I was a teenager, all the guys used to pile into Bob Kaiser's car and go to a nearby college gym to play basketball. How good it felt to be part of the group and share in the anticipation of the ballplaying coming up! Back then, sports narrowed my focus in comforting ways. I could deal with basketball and nothing else. I didn't have to attend to everything that was going on in my life, some of which wasn't all that pleasant. On those occasions, I didn't have to deal with uncertainty or make a lot of decisions. Basketball was predictable, I knew how it would go. No pain, no surprises.

As it turned out, once the Griffins and Brian got to the park, we never got around to actually *playing* baseball. Instead, we practiced. First, the four children fanned out and took some infield practice, which included turning some snappy double plays and making quick flips to third to catch imaginary runners foolish enough to try to advance on a ground ball. Then the three boys clustered in left field and gathered in some fly balls and pegged them home to me, the catcher—or, in 7-year-old Neil's case, hit the cut-off person, his big sister Erin. I smile now as I think of fearless, determined little Neil that afternoon. He was something out of the old *Bad News Bears* movie: holding a 28-inch bat down at the end (no choking up for him!), scooting after grounders and snaring some in stunning fashion while others whizzed past him, racing after fly balls that would whap into his floppy oversized glove and set him into a spin, and throwing so hard his legs would go out from under him and then bouncing up as if he were on a trampoline. He seemed to be having the time of his life.

After outfield drills we took some batting practice, with each of us getting in about twenty swings. I had the job of throwing batting practice to Erin (the 14-year-old). Erin stood up to the plate with a stern look on her face, holding the bat high in a right-handed stance. She was wearing jeans and sneakers and a blue jersey from her school soccer team with a white number 22 and "Griffin" on the back. I did the best I could to toss the ball softly down the middle, although, truth be told, accurate throwing has never been my strong suit. It quickly became apparent that things weren't going well for either Erin or me. The infrequent times I managed to get the ball over the plate, Erin either missed altogether or produced buntlike dribblers. Things seemed to get deadly silent around us. No one was saying anything. The wind even seemed to stop making noise. Erin tried a different bat with no better results. I could see she was getting frustrated and upset, which in turn made me self-conscious and tense, and it got even tougher for me to get the ball over. I started short-arming it as if I were throwing darts, and that just made things worse.

Finally, action on the field was suspended while Erin and her dad conferred at home plate. I couldn't hear what was said, but I can guess, because I was relieved on the mound and assigned the duty of handling incoming throws for the pitcher. That helped the situation a bit, but Erin still didn't produce more than three or four dribblers to short and some weak pop flies to the right side of the infield. She looked defeated as she tossed down her bat, and Leif took his turn to hit. I felt bad for Erin. I felt I had let her down by not doing a better job of pitching. I reflected briefly on my lifelong affliction with a scatter arm.

Thirteen-year-old Leif, lean and athletic-looking with his baseball cap pulled low over his blond hair, is deadly serious about sports. He is an avid soccer player—he attended a soccer camp later that summer—and he plays organized baseball in a youth league. He is a huge fan of the Minnesota Twins (this was Minneapolis, remember). That afternoon at the park he was all business; it could have been the seventh game of the World Series. He swung mightily at the ball. He soberly gobbled up grounders and smoked them over to first, demonstrating a remarkable arm for someone his age. When he whiffed or fouled one off at bat or kicked one in the field, I could see that to him it was no small matter.

I was left with the distinct impression that Leif saw a great deal on the line that afternoon, and that this activity was much closer to work than play for him. I sensed that in his eyes he was undergoing a test of sorts, and for him there was the question of whether he was going to measure up. He was performing for his dad, his buddy Brian, and former ballplayer Uncle Bob. (I have a strong hunch my sports exploits have been puffed up to him far beyond their actual merits.) I understand that Leif has mentioned hoping to get a college scholarship someday to play baseball. Later in the summer, I was informed by my brother that the family and some other relatives had gone to see one of Leif's youth league games. Leif had gone hitless at the plate and was feeling really bad about it, and in effect had apologized for his failure to everyone who had come to the game.

I am sure that there was more going on in this sports activity with Erin, Leif, and Neil than simply a chance to have some innocent fun and be together with the family and their relative from back east. And that brings me to the point of this chapter and an idea that is a basis for much of this book: *for kids, sports is often about more than just having a good time and developing physical skills.* For many children, sports is an arena for taking on the most crucial challenges they face during this time of their lives. Although the meaning of sports for most children is largely tacit or inarticulate, nevertheless they sense that sports has the potential to be more than simple recreation. The investigation of sports and children is no trivial matter. For the child who participates, and particularly for the child who participates avidly, sports is about growing up, the direction life will take for this child. Sports can have a significant effect on the success or failure of that process.

Sports is certainly not unique in this regard. School, for example, is more than a place for learning. It too is a playing field where, for better or worse, vital personal issues are resolved—resolutions that not only can have a major impact on the child's life in the present but also can have a significant effect on the resolutions of the adult issues coming up (love, family and friendship, work, connections to the society, personal happiness). In my view, the potential of sports for having an impact on matters of this import is what most compels parents' attention to their children's involvement in it.

It is inaccurate to say that sports inevitably has a particular significance for children or that participation in sports necessarily results in a particular outcome for them. To get at the meaning of sports for children and to understand its effect on them it is necessary to take into account what each child is like as an individual, his or her personal history, and his or her stage of life. We must also recognize and understand the child's circumstances—at home, in school, and with friends—and the ways the child deals with these circumstances. Finally, we need to understand the society and culture children live in and its effect on them.

Saying that, I am not implying that sports is a neutral activity that children simply make of as they will. Sports is not a blank canvas on which a child paints a picture. Indeed, one of the major premises of this book is that we must look closely at the character or essence of sports in order to determine the directions in which it pushes the children who participate. In fact, the best way to view sports is as an *exchange* between a certain child and a certain sports activity in a certain place and at a certain time, and with certain other people. In order to understand or predict the outcomes of that exchange, we have to explore both parties in the interaction, the child and the sport situation.

An exploration of the concerns and issues inherent in this time in a child's life—the *agenda of childhood*, if you will—can contribute to your insight into the possible consequences of sports for your child as he or she grows up. The period of childhood I want to discuss in the pages that follow extends from roughly the ages of 6 through 18. I will describe a number of dimensions of growing up. These items have *developmental* significance. They are developmental because they have to do with the way an individual develops as viewed from the perspective of the most basic interlinked changes that occur over the span of his or her life. Their existence and interplay constitute the template or design of this stage of life. It is into this reality that sports fits and has its most significant impact on children, and it is within this frame that the effects of sports can best be analyzed.[1]

The agenda of childhood is made up of the following items or elements:

- Personal Autonomy
- Gender Identity
- Personal Mastery
- Physical Development
- Mental Development
- Self-Concept
- Moral Development
- Self-Esteem
- Character
- Social Development
- Academic Development
- Self-Respect
- Personality
- Personal Philosophy

- Personal Identity
- Social Exchange, Fun, Excitement, and Challenge
- Relationship with Parents

In the pages that follow, along with a description of each item of the agenda of childhood, I will offer my own comments and, in some instances, refer to research and writings that bear on this area. In some cases, I will begin the discussion here and continue it in later chapters.

PERSONAL AUTONOMY

Beginning as early as 2 years of age, children seek to control their own behavior and establish feelings of personal autonomy. As they get older they become increasingly aware of their ability to initiate activities and manage themselves, as well as the limitations and constraints placed on this capacity. Getting in charge of one's own life, free from outside control, moving ahead on one's own initiative, is a central task of childhood. This contrasts with being reactive, passive, inactive, dependent, hesitant. Most of us can distinguish between those two orientations in children when we see them.

Sports can be the setting for the development of autonomy and initiative. However, the emphasis is on *can* be, not *will* be. Some sports contexts foster independence and an action orientation, whereas others foster dependence and inertia. Some sports settings breed a sense of industry among children, whereas others promote feelings of ineffectiveness. For example, a child's sense of autonomy is closely linked to the ability to choose. Therefore, a highly structured setting with a dominant coach and rigidly prescribed roles could win in the sports arena and lose in the developmental arena. The point is that sports situations differ from one another, and we must assess them one by one in terms of precisely what we care about. Two football teams may be similar in football and at the same time very different in the game of growing up—and becoming one's own person is a vital part of that latter game.

GENDER IDENTITY

Before the age of 3, children begin to understand whether they are boys or girls and they begin to take on gender identities and roles. They learn how important the meaning of gender is for themselves, including others' perceptions of them and attitudes toward them. Adolescence brings a continued elaboration of one's gender identity. With the arrival of puberty, it more explicitly includes a sexual component. *What are boys (or girls) like ideally, and what am I like specifically, and how do I act accordingly? What is my relationship, including sexual, to members of the opposite sex and to my own? How attractive am I to those in whom I have a sexual interest, and how could I be more appealing to them?*

Does sports contribute to particular gender identities? I believe so. Directly and indirectly, sports sends messages to participants about masculinity and femininity and sexuality, and it provides a context for acting consistently with these messages. I think of Judy Oppenheimer's comment (the mother of the high school football player I mentioned in Chapter 1) that she wanted her son to be "big, booming, triumphant—a warrior" and how she went on to say that sports made her son into one.[2] But even if sports helps produce them, do we want big booming warriors? Many would say that is precisely what we *don't* want or need, that we have too many insensitive, violence-prone Neanderthals posing as men as it is. Others, however, think we could use more warriors these days. They believe they see an overabundance of soft-bodied, self-conscious, edgeless, somehow emasculated, overly domesticated, and ineffectual nice guys—men for whom even the thought of being either booming or triumphant makes them crave another glass of white wine to calm themselves down.

Here is a question I have asked myself since beginning work on this book: Has the increased participation of girls and women in athletics led to a healthy broadening of the definition of what it means to be female, or has it promoted an inappropriate blurring of the differences between the sexes? Is sports telling young women that to be successful they have to emulate men? There is much talk these days about girls being socialized into an overly narrow gender definition in contrast to boys, who, it is thought, are given wider latitude to experiment with ways of being male. On the contrary, I observe many parents (and society generally) proudly supporting girls in what once would have been called boy-type activities. Perhaps this is because today's culture places less value on being what has traditionally been seen as feminine, and perhaps it comes in some part from the view that girls are likely to have to compete hard in the work world later on. In any case, the result seems to be that girls are in fact more readily encouraged to be on the Little League team than boys are to take ballet lessons or to figure skate, activities that parents may worry will make boys appear, or actually become, weak or effeminate. In Chapter 6, I explore gender issues more fully.

PERSONAL MASTERY

Children develop perceptions of their own levels of competence, perseverance, and effectiveness. Whether the child achieves a sense of personal mastery is a crucial issue in middle childhood, roughly age 8 to 11, although it is a continuing concern during adolescence. Children come to see themselves either as doers who get things accomplished or, in contrast, ineffectual people.[3]

A child's view of himself or herself as a masterful person (not a perfect person, or someone who can do everything well, just one who is fundamentally efficacious) is strongly affected by the outcomes he or she obtains when doing things that he or she accepts as important. Children are an audience to themselves. From the age of 7 or so, they draw conclusions about themselves based on the results of their efforts. Sports teams and situations hold up different standards of achievement to participants and differ in the likelihood that a child's efforts will meet with success and positive acknowledgment. The question becomes this: If kids take sports seriously and do not achieve good outcomes in their own eyes and in the eyes of others, what impact will this have on their feeling of masterfulness, and how will it affect the way they approach other areas of their lives now and in the future? I will revisit this question at the end of the chapter.

PHYSICAL DEVELOPMENT

Children develop in physical capability and acquire a perspective toward themselves as physical beings. They may come to cherish and enhance themselves physically and integrate their physicality into their total being. Alternatively, without the proper influences they may come to ignore, neglect, or abuse this dimension of themselves. Physical activity is necessary to build motor skills, and organized sports can be that activity, although so too can bicycling, skiing, and throwing a Frisbee. It seems clear that there is a pace to keep in mind: pushing children to acquire physical skills more quickly than developmentally appropriate and emphasizing comparisons with older youths can lessen children's optimism about their own abilities and thereby stifle their motivation to use and expand on their physical abilities.

As for the effect of sports on the way youngsters view and treat their bodies, I have seen it go both ways. I have known athletes who respected and nurtured their bodies. I have known athletes who considered their bodies an integral part of their being. But I have also known athletes—teenagers, not just adults—who viewed their bodies merely as tools, tools they often abused. I refer to risking their health and safety recklessly, playing in spite of injury, and taking drugs to stimulate performance and stay in competition in spite of injury. I have known athletes who scrutinized everything that went into their bodies to make sure it was good for them, and others who attacked their bodies with junk food, nicotine, alcohol, and so-called recreational drugs. I have known athletes who stayed in shape as an end in itself, and I have known athletes who let themselves go soft the minute the competition ended. Some sports situations promote treating one's body well, whereas others foster the objectification and mistreatment of one's body. What happens in a particular child's case is the result of the interplay between what that child is like and what the sports circumstance is like. As a parent, you need to monitor and assess this interplay as it involves your own child.

MENTAL DEVELOPMENT

A crucial task of childhood is to mature mentally. Fundamentally, mental (other terms, intellectual, cognitive) development is growth in one's capability to think abstractly.[4] It is the ability to use one's mind effectively: to reason, to analyze, to create, to solve problems, and to make assessments, and then to use the results of one's thinking to guide one's actions. Some situations teach children things and help them learn to do things, but at the same time they don't promote children's ability and tendency to think hard and perceptively for themselves, which, it must be underscored, involves more than the ability to make quick and clever decisions and responses, or merely employ tactics necessary to carry out a strategy determined by someone else.

A question for parents to consider is whether sports activities go beyond contributing to their child's knowledge and skill and ability to cope with immediate situations to developing his or her intellect. Personally, I wouldn't make the claim that sports characteristically helps a child develop his or her mental capability in the way I have defined it here. In fact, my impression is that in most instances sports does not serve that end to any significant degree.

SELF-CONCEPT

During childhood, children develop an increasingly clear picture of themselves. Self-concept is a decision one makes about oneself: *This is what describes me. This is what I am interested in. This is what I am good at and not good at. These are the kind of things I do and don't do. This is how others see me and treat me.* The experiences of childhood and adolescence help draw the outlines and fill in the details of one's self-image, including whether it is favorable or unfavorable.

A child's self-concept is very important because it provides him or her with a frame of reference that guides future thoughts and actions.

For example: *I'm not trying out for the debate team because that is not what I do. I wouldn't get much out of that. Debate doesn't square with who I am and what I am good at and like to do. But I am going to check out football because that's more me.* In this case, debate didn't happen, and not because of some external force preventing or discouraging it, but rather because of an internal guide or screen that exists within the child—the child's self-concept. Self-concepts can be both useful and get in children's way. They are useful when they direct children toward involvements that are appropriate for them. They get in the way to the extent that children's view of themselves stops them from doing something that would have been enjoyable, enriching, and productive.

For children who participate, sports doesn't end with the last tick of the scoreboard clock. Sports persists inside them as memories and feelings and conclusions, and all this gets translated into a generalized conception of themselves. Very important, to an extent depending on the meaning children attribute to their involvement, playing sports contributes to and reinforces their self-concept in areas beyond the sports-related part of their self-definition. The question for you, of course, is how sports is affecting your child's overall self-concept.

MORAL DEVELOPMENT

Over time, children become moral people. They take on a sense of right and wrong. They acquire perspectives on fairness and justice and the rights of others. They become concerned about others and feel responsible for their welfare—or they don't. They become kind and decent and tolerant people—or they don't. They become good people or bad people. They become honest or dishonest people. Children learn morality through their interactions with others and from the examples of people around them and from the activities they engage in.

Along with everything else it is, sports is a moral teacher, and we have to assess it on that basis. Here are some questions to ask about your child's sports involvement: *At the most basic level, what do these people believe in? What values does this place, this activity, reflect? How would I feel if my child became the embodiment of what this sports setting believes to be right?* Reflect on these questions now, and consider what I have to offer on this topic in Chapter 4.

SELF-ESTEEM

Self-esteem is an aspect of self-concept. It refers to one's own assessment of two particular dimensions of oneself: (1) one's *worth,* and (2) one's *competence* (or masterfulness as described above).[5] People with high self-esteem see themselves as basically valuable. In their own eyes, they matter. They deserve good treatment. They deserve to be happy. They deserve to live well. Those who possess high self-esteem more than like themselves. They count. Their dignity counts. Their life counts. People with high self-esteem consider themselves capable of getting important things done. They are confident. They proceed from the assumption that they can accomplish what they set out to accomplish. People with high self-esteem presume that they will produce good results and not have to settle for reasons or excuses for why they didn't. Positive self-esteem is crucial to living well. If you don't believe you are a deserving and capable person, you operate from a rickety underpinning when trying to construct a satisfying and productive life. You are likely to construct a life befitting someone who isn't deserving and isn't effective.

Conventional wisdom says that sports contributes positively to self-esteem. However, the literature and research I have reviewed doesn't offer much support for the idea. One author reports that varsity sports tends to increase self-esteem slightly for boys but not for girls.[6] Another researcher found that even though playing football raises boys' self-esteem a bit, the increase is not statistically significant (i.e., the increase wasn't great enough to allow him to conclude anything definitively).[7] It is important to ask how these writers define self-esteem and how they arrived at their conclusions—it wasn't clear from their writings. Self-esteem, as I defined it earlier, refers to a general or overall sense of one's worth and capability. Personally, I have seen athletes who thought little of themselves anywhere but on the athletic field, and sometimes not even there. Some people who win every wrestling match think that is about all they are good for. What about the wrestlers who win very few matches, or are on the team but rarely or never get to compete? True self-esteem is to a great extent the result of accomplishment. It is a byproduct of success. It is not enough to have others tell you how great you are, or for you to tell it to yourself, if you don't have objective evidence. A fact of life is that you have to earn self-esteem through your own achievements and the obstacles you overcome.

Although I believe sports can significantly affect a child's self-esteem, at this point I am not ready to say that simply participating in sports can be counted on to boost it. Sports can enhance children's sense of their own overall worth and capability, but it can also detract from it. Comparison—asking oneself, "How do I stack up against others in my group?"—is a major vehicle for determining personal worth. The question that particularly concerns me is this: What happens to the self-esteem of children who don't measure up well to the accomplishments of other athletes on their team? Also, it gives me pause to see the expressed or unexpressed message (especially in sports for older kids) that no matter who you are, the team comes first, that no one is bigger than the team, that every individual is expendable; you are replaceable and don't forget it. Moreover, consider the common sports credo that no matter how much you accomplish, it will never be enough, so don't get comfortable with your own capabilities or achievements. More than many people imagine, organized sports is frequently a training ground, even for star athletes, for self-effacement ("I'm just one among many," "I'm not good enough") rather than self-esteem.

Parents need to ask: *What exactly is it about a sports experience that enhances participants' self-worth and confidence in themselves?* These concerns will come up again later on. Meanwhile ask yourself: *What is sports doing for my child's self-esteem?*

CHARACTER

There are many definitions of character. They include such personal qualities as responsibility, persistence, courage, self-discipline, honesty, integrity, the willingness to work hard, compassion for others, generosity, independence, and tolerance. I think it is fair to say that nothing more defines a person than the level of his or her character. Childhood and adolescence is, as much as anything, a time of character formation.

Sports has long held a reputation for building character. I will explore the evidence and share my assessment of the relationship between sports and character in Chapter 4. In the meantime, I invite you to think about it: *What effect is sports having, or do I anticipate it having, on my child's character? What effect would I like it to have?* [8]

SOCIAL DEVELOPMENT

Over the course of childhood, children develop as social beings. Social development includes a concern for social skills, sociability, and prosocial and antisocial attitudes. Social development comprises such things as friendship, social ranking, status, power, rejection and acceptance, inclusion and exclusion, dominance and submission, leadership, connection to the group, cooperativeness, aggression and passivity and withdrawal, and conflict. It also includes social insightfulness: the ability to infer the intentions of others and discern why things happen as they do in social contexts. [9]

Defining one's relationship to the social world outside the family involves the resolution of some crucial questions: *What am I like socially? Where do I fit? With whom?* As children get older and more mobile and mentally better able to take others into account, the peer group becomes an increasingly significant part of their lives. Puberty exacerbates this process. Children take on and are assigned (the individual/context interaction idea again) status and social roles: leader, follower, cool guy, social star, everyone's friend, and so on. Then there are the social identities that are defined by their relation to the group: part of the crowd, outsider-trying-to-get-in, loner, and the rest. In particular, adolescents are at a time in their lives when they are looking for a way to be that will meet with approval and acceptance. As most adults can still recall, issues of inclusion and exclusion are big concerns during early and later adolescence. These are the years when it becomes a big thing to be in the right crowd. *What does the group think of me?* I remember worrying in high school that I wouldn't have anyone to eat lunch with. What a relief when I spotted my sports buddies and they said, "Hey Griff, come on over."

Research has shown that sports is a major determinant of friendship patterns and social standing among children and adolescents. For many youngsters, sports is a—if not *the*—primary context for social development. Sports often determines who children are around and thus what social examples they observe and who responds approvingly and disapprovingly to their social initiatives. Recently I was in a high school cafeteria and remarked to myself how the athletes segregated themselves by sex and by sport at the tables. In school, sports can be a major vehicle for obtaining social rewards such as recognition, praise, and adulation. Studies have shown that both boys and girls think of participation in sports as the best way to achieve popularity. (Interestingly, being on the honor roll is considered the least promising way.)[10] Many children see sports as *the* way to make it socially. You can imagine how high the stakes are for these individuals to be successful at sports, and what the personal costs can be if they aren't.

Like all contexts, sports is not neutral but rather favors certain social ways and arrangements. Ask yourself: *How is my child defined socially in this sports situation? Where is he or she placed in the social scheme of things? What is he or she learning about being with others, with groups, in this sports setting? What are the social models and ideals in this circumstance? What kind of social being is my child there? How does that square with my hopes for my child, and with his or her hopes for him or herself?*

ACADEMIC DEVELOPMENT

Academic development involves the entire range of things a young person learns or attains in school: particular knowledge and skills, attitudes and orientations toward school and learning and the life of the mind, effectiveness as a student (i.e., how well a youngster can do what it takes to be successful in school), academic achievement (grades, awards, and other scholastic recognition), and the level of encouragement and support the student receives from the school.

As for the connection between sports involvement and a child's academic orientation and success, I explore this in Chapter 3. In Chapter 5, I explore the role of sports in schools and what effect that has on the children who attend them—even those who do not participate in sports. Chapter 9 considers schools in relationship to what I term the *culture of achievement.* For now, reflect on the fact that sports is such a powerful force in the eyes of young people that one study showed that if forced to choose, both high school boys and girls preferred success in sports over success in the classroom. In another study, a majority of young people stated that they wanted to be remembered as athletic stars rather than as brilliant students.[11] Still other research reported that boys tend to find failure in sports to be more aversive than failure in academics.[12]

SELF-RESPECT

An issue throughout life, but especially pressing in adolescence, is the achievement of self-respect.[13] People who are self-respecting are more themselves, more authentic, in their lives. They place stronger demands on themselves to get on with creating a satisfying and honorable life. They avoid negative talk and self-pity and take action stemming from the intention—not just the hope—of achieving their aims in life. Without respect for ourselves, it is tough to be happy in our lives.[14] By happiness I mean a deep, pervasive, lasting sense that "Yes, life is good," in contrast to transitory pleasures or "up" times. As a practical matter, self-respect and happiness go hand and hand. We are a watchful audience to ourselves from the age of 7 or 8 onward, and we can't get away from ourselves no matter how hard some of us try (through alcohol and drugs, amusements, consumption, rationalizations, and the rest). We have to live a life that we can respect, because even if no one else notices, even if others buy our line, we are witnessing ourselves and we won't accept our excuses or get distracted by our act.

My view is that we earn self-respect in certain ways—that is to say, there are rules for attaining self-respect. First, we have to assume personal responsibility for accomplishing important things. We don't get away with ducking responsibility or holding others accountable for our fate. Second, we have to be productive. We have to achieve positive results when we take on valued undertakings. When we do that, others respect our responsibility and the results we achieve. We note their respect for us as well as observe our own accomplishments and accord ourselves respect. We don't have to be responsible and successful every time or be at the top of the heap to be respected and self-respecting, but we can't fail every time either. If we continually come up short at what we and those who matter to us consider significant tasks, it is extremely difficult to achieve or maintain respect for ourselves.

Sports' contribution to the attainment of self-respect is a crucial matter for thought and investigation. Again, sometimes sports contributes to a child's self-respect and sometimes it doesn't. Given what I have said, is sports a context in which your child is growing in self-respect?

PERSONALITY

Individuals take on or sharpen their personalities during their youth. By personality I mean a person's style, manner, persona, the way he presents himself. I consider personality to be the product of a combination of factors: individual choice, modeling (emulating others), conditioning (training, outside shaping), and one's inherent nature.

Sports is a way to represent oneself to the world. Spend time in any close-knit athletic context and you'll see that a certain kind, or a few kinds, of personality profiles are the most prevalent and most favored there. Athletes feel a push toward being certain ways and receive rewards (approval, acceptance) for doing so. Listen to athletes being interviewed on television and see if you don't notice a similar manner among many of them. Undoubtedly this is due to the fact that certain types of people are drawn to sports in the first place, but it goes beyond that. There is personality-shaping going on; or so it seems, anyway.

If your child is deeply involved in sports and you notice he or she is starting to act differently, it could have something to do with the cues your child is picking up from sports—coaches, fellow players, athletes on television, and so on. Your child may be imitating a professional or college sports hero, or taking on the personality of the star of the team he or she is on: *If it works for him, it might work for me.* Of course, it may be a fleeting phenomenon, but then again childhood is a particularly formative time of life, when even short-lived behaviors have the potential of cementing themselves into one's personality for a good time to come.

The "sports persona" can take at least three forms. (I'm thinking here of boys.) First, there's the flat, laconic style. It is a kind of a Clint Eastwood approach. Stay detached and don't say anything unless you have to. Keep it brief and don't get too effusive or animated about anything. Just play your position and don't be shooting off your mouth. Then there is the humble, deferring, "no rough edges" manner: "I accept this award on behalf of my teammates, because if it weren't for them . . ." These ways of presenting oneself have a somewhat mechanical, clipped, terse, rehearsed quality. And there is the devil-may-care, Budweiser-commercial, beers-with-the-guys type. Of course athletes reflect the full spectrum of personal styles, but the sports culture does seem to favor certain styles and nudge participants in that direction. I have noticed that verbally expansive, analytical, self-revealing personalities don't often appear in the physically-oriented, no-nonsense sports world. Whether this is because people of this bent are changed by the sports world or simply seldom enter it remains an open question.

PERSONAL PHILOSOPHY

As children get older, increasingly they think about what is worth believing in and using to guide the conduct of their lives. Even though it may still be quite primitive, children begin early to develop a philosophy of life—a set of explanations and ideals and priorities that give them direction. Political orientations and allegiances are articulated. Attitudes toward society and art and other people are clarified. Personal aspirations are defined: *This is where I am going in my life.* For some—perhaps too few these days—these are the years of fantasizing about being a hero, or accomplishing great deeds, or being part of a great cause. Personal values are crucial to all these processes. Values answer the questions: *What is preferable? What has merit? What is right?*

Sports is a place where children work through issues of belief and value. And again, sports is not a neutral context. Sports represents certain ideas and ideals, and fosters their acceptance among those who participate in it. Later on, in Chapters 4 and 9 and elsewhere, I will talk more about this.

PERSONAL IDENTITY

In contrast to younger children, teenagers are better able to think abstractly and therefore are more capable of reflecting on what they are like and, most important, what they *should* be like as individuals.

They resolve the questions: *Who am I? What do I do that distinguishes me from others? What makes me special? How can I show people who I am?* The term that is used to refer to this process is *identity formation*.[15] For the most part, *personal identity* is another term for self-concept, except that it has a stronger connotation of one's place in the overall scheme of things, the niche one fills in the world. Central in this process, along with development of *gender identity* as described earlier, the teenage years build on the beginnings of a *work identity* acquired when younger. Early in life, children come to a global sense of the sort of worker they are (*I am a good worker; I do what my parents and the teacher say; I work hard; I am a screw-up*). With adolescence, young people typically give some fairly serious thought and experimentation to the particular kind of work they do, or might do in the future, that can define them as individuals and members of the group: *I do this kind of work and not that kind, and that says who I am.* For some children, sports takes on the nature of work and thereby to a greater or lesser degree helps mold their work identity.

In good part, children learn about who they are from what others in their world and their involvements inform them about themselves. Sports contexts tell the children who participate who they are in relation to what this setting most values in a person. In this way, sports is more than a game to play; it is a lesson in identity. Contributing to the strong influence sports can have is its capacity to become who children are, subsume their being. Some children don't just *play* sports, they *are* athletes. That is who they are to themselves, and that is who they are to others.

All groups encourage their members to minimize their differences with one another. Group members are presumably drawn to the group because they have something in common in the first place, but the dynamic of the group draws them toward even more closely approximating each other, whether it is in appearance, values, or behavior. The individual self becomes depersonalized in deference to the group identity and one's place in the group. Group behaviors, attitudes, and skills and the personal qualities most valued and needed by the group become the norm for the individual to follow. At the same time individuals are pressured to minimize differences with others in the group, they are also encouraged to maximize them with the outgroup, which is to say, everyone else. The result is group think and group polarization, as well as a strong desire for acceptance and status in the group. Insularity grows out of such settings. Whenever there is competition or perceived threat, there will be pressure for members to assume a group identity in contrast to a personal identity and to converge in norms and behavior. They start to take on similar language, gestures, and dress; individuality is diminished.[16] Clearly, the competitive nature of sports provides an extra push toward commonality among its participants.

Adolescents have dual desires. They seek inclusion and interdependence. And they want—and need—a sense of their own independence and uniqueness. At best, children manage to integrate these goals, but there are times when they remain in contradiction. For example, in sports and elsewhere, personal autonomy can be sacrificed or hindered by the desire to fit in, and individuality can run up against the pressure to play the role that best serves the group. Often I have heard coaches lecture their athletes, "Remember, there is no I in team." There may be no I in team, but there certainly is the need for an I in life if one is to live *his* or *her* own life and not just *a* life.

The balance between the needs of the individual and the interests of the group is a major concern of mine. There is no place where this polarity is more obvious than in children's and adolescents' sports activities. What happens to a young person's sense of individuality and uniqueness when confronted with a setting that tells him he must subordinate his interests to those of the team? Recently I talked with a high school basketball coach who had benched a couple of his senior starters. His rationale was that even though the seniors were better than those who replaced them, the team was having a losing season and the program would be better next year and beyond if the younger players got some experience. I wondered about the rights and welfare of the seniors, what was fair to those kids, and how their needs balanced off against the coach's interests and the welfare of the team as an entity that has a history and that continues after these individuals have gone their separate ways.

It is clear that youngsters look to individuals in their group who are held up as exemplary for answers to questions such as: *Who is truly admirable? Why? How can I become more like that?* Sports, like other groups, holds up examples of individuals for children to admire and emulate. For children caught up in sports, prominent athletes are the people they look up to. Star athletes become heroes, more than doctors or artists or businesspeople or religious leaders. We need to ask ourselves: *Just who are these athletic heroes? What do their lives represent? What are the values of these admired athletes? How are their values related to academics and learning? What is their record of achievement in school? What is their orientation toward work? For that matter, what exactly is the work of playing sports for a living? What does professional sports say about the nature of work? What moral examples do star athletes provide young people? What are their attitudes toward the opposite sex? What does the example of athletics say about how to achieve a good life in this society? What is a good life according to these athletes?* There is no more important question for a society to explore than whom its children admire and why.

SOCIAL EXCHANGE, FUN, EXCITEMENT, CHALLENGE

Experiencing social exchange, fun, excitement, and personal challenge are major *motivations* of youngsters. As inherently social beings, most children find being around other kids rewarding in itself. Also, children are drawn to anything that provides fun and excitement. Finally, they like a challenge, a hill to climb, figuratively or literally. Children may say they want things to be easy, but they don't, not really, not deep down.

Sports is an activity that serves these motivations. Sports is a way to be with others, and it challenges its participants, and it is often fun and exciting. For some children there is little else other than sports that offers the possibility of these kinds of experiences. So if you want to know why kids get into sports, those are likely to be among the reasons. And if you want to replace sports with something else, you have a guide as to what your task is: either help your children find other involvements that give them a chance to socialize or that are challenging or fun or give them a charge, or help them identify other motivations that can lead to personal satisfaction, such as personal expression or self-improvement or service to others.

RELATIONSHIP WITH PARENTS

Besides the effect of sports on children's relationships with their peers, it has an impact on their relationships with their parents. Organized sports can bring children and their parents together as they share in the activity, the child playing and the parents watching and supporting, but it can also divide them. If you are the parent of a committed young athlete, you know how athletics can consume a young person's life to the point that it crowds out family life. There are practices and games. There are clinics and off-season leagues. Most sports can be (and to be really good in them, have to be) engaged in year-round. Then there is the study and weight training, and all the sports reading and time spent thinking and talking about sports. Apart from the effect on family life, leading scholars call for the need for diversity in children's lives.[17] When sports gets to the point that it significantly closes off other involvements, it becomes a matter for concern.

Children, and adolescents in particular, want independence, but they also want to please their parents and make their parents proud of them. In extreme cases, sports can be the way to win the respect and approval of Mom and Dad. Often children feel pressure from their parents to play sports, and more than that, to excel in them. They sometimes feel pressure to perform in sports to the level of their parents' expectations. Some children may actually think that a good relationship with their parents is contingent on their continued involvement in sports and the quality of their play. For some children, it is almost as if they are taking care of their parents by playing sports, providing something they perceive their parents as needing. Some children are in an unenviable bind: if they don't do well in sports, they disappoint their parents; and if they do do well, then they are treated by their parents like budding professional athletes instead of children.

You want the best for your children and that they be happy and well. But you also want to maintain a good relationship with them—and you have a right to want that, and the right to work to create and maintain that. You don't want your children to be alienated from you or disrespectful to you or dismissive of you and what you represent. Even though you want them to be their own people, at the same time you don't want to lose them. Sports has to be assessed in terms of its impact on your relationship with your children. You matter too.

SUMMARY

This, then, is what I consider to be the agenda of childhood. Youngsters are dealing with issues of autonomy and initiative, and mastery. They are confronting questions regarding gender. They are learning how to use their minds, to think. They are establishing a relationship with themselves as physical, corporeal entities. They are defining who they are as individuals, which includes assuming a work identity. They are developing a social identity and social skills and a place in the social world. They are finding beliefs and values to guide them. They are becoming moral beings. They are shaping their personalities and character. They are achieving self-esteem and self-respect (or not). They are finding people to be with and creating some fun and excitement in their lives. They are attending school and developing an academic style and academic skills and compiling an academic record. They are identifying scholastic and career ambitions and laying the groundwork for further education or training. And they are establishing a particular kind of relationship with their parent or parents.

While children work through this agenda of childhood in many venues, including the classroom and the streetcorner, organized sports is a particularly good vehicle for it. Sports is a public endeavor: people are watching. The fact that people are looking on increases youngsters' self-awareness and self-attention, and this they find rewarding because with all their identity concerns this is a particularly self-referenced time of life. It feels right to children for the light to be shining on them, to be pushed to attend to their developing selves, and, as they act on these developmental issues, to have their actions receive immediate public validation. Also, in sports there are usually clear criteria for success and failure. You know how you are doing and when you are making progress. Add to that the fact that sports is arousing and enjoyable when so much of what is in children's worlds isn't. Researchers have asked children why they participate in sports, and the agenda of childhood is reflected in their responses. Reasons children gave included the following: the opportunity to learn and improve skills; the chance to meet others, to make friends and be part of a group; excitement and personal challenge; achievement and status; fitness, energy and tension release; and fun. Boys tended to be more motivated by achievement and status than girls, who participated more for fun and friendship.[18]

It is important to keep in mind that children don't choose sports as a vehicle to serve their needs totally of their own accord. They are socialized into it by their parents, their peers, the media, and their school. Children choose what to do from the options they know about and that seem available. It is as if they carry an album of pictures in their heads, and when they are faced with deciding what to do they call up the album and pick the most appealing picture and then try to bring it to life.[19] Various elements of this society provide pictures for children. A few years ago, the media presented the picture of skater Nancy Kerrigan overcoming a physical assault intended to keep her out of the competition and, amid incredible public interest (including the rapt attention of proud parents—a fantasy for most children), skating to a silver medal in the Winter Olympics. We can only speculate how many little girls put that picture in their mental album and the impact it has had on their lives.

Now, back to my niece and nephews, Erin, Neil, and Leif, and our day in the park. My guess is to the extent that the experience was about more than catching and hitting baseballs, its meaning for them lies somewhere in what I have just discussed. It was a chance to be part of a social experience and to have some fun, but likely it was more than that. For 7-year-old Neil, it could have had to do with being included in the group and autonomy and initiative and personal mastery. For 13-year-old Leif, the activity could have touched on issues of self-definition. It could be that Leif has decided to build an identity as an athlete. If he has, that will have consequences far beyond the scores of the games in which he participates and his athletic performances. Perhaps for 14-year-old Erin, the afternoon at the park brought up issues regarding gender. As I think about it now, there was no acknowledgment on that occasion that Erin is a girl. It was a unisex world that day. Erin was dressed exactly like the boys, and as far as I could tell there was no difference in expectations for her and the boys. I don't know what difference, if any, it made to her, but it may have made some.

Any of the other factors I have outlined above may have been involved as well. The sports experience could have had an impact on the three as social beings and on their personalities. In a small way it could have had an impact on their self-esteem and self-respect. It could have had an impact on their relationship with others in their family and with me. I don't want to make too much of this occasion, but I think if you add its effect to the outcomes of all the other direct contacts the children have had and will have with sports, in school and on the playground, plus their indirect experiences from reading about sports and watching it on television, it could well amount to something of significance in their lives.

CONCLUSION: THE IMPORTANCE OF SUCCESS

With the agenda of childhood as the frame of reference, it appears that sports can be both a setting for the successful resolution of the developmental issues of childhood and the venue of the failure to achieve healthy maturation. Sports can build up a child, and it can diminish a child. One significant conclusion I have reached in this regard is that, in general, to the degree a child gets invested in sports, it is important that he or she be successful in them. Not just participate in sports, but *do well* in them. By doing well, I mean matching up to the particular sport's own standards. If its standard is to have a high batting average, then I mean having a high batting average. I devote Chapters 8 and 9 to an exploration of how as a parent you can contribute to your child's success in sports. If sports is a big thing to a parent or child, and the child isn't good at it, I think sports can be damaging to the child. That message doesn't play well to many parents I suppose. It would be a lot easier for me to say, "Go ahead, encourage your children to participate in sports. Sports will be good for them, get them with other kids, teach them about teamwork and sticking with it." But that is not the way I see it. In sports, or school or anywhere else in life, the best circumstance for children to be in is where they confront challenges just beyond their current personal capability and are successful in meeting them. The ideal is for children to have to work hard, put in their utmost effort, and then achieve measurable improvement and success. And then for the others in that situation to show them that they respect both their hard work and the good results they obtained. A major responsibility of parents is to help their children identify areas where their efforts will meet with success.

I am not optimistic that many young people can imagine or act on criteria for success beyond those inherent in the particular circumstance they are in. Children are new to the world and do not yet have the tools to mediate the forces coming at them. If children see sports as an important part of their lives, then their success and failure in that context, their accomplishments and the degree to which their efforts are appreciated by others, can significantly affect their view of themselves, their aspirational levels, and their achievements in other areas. All of this can affect their future, because everything in life is of a piece: what happens up the line is connected to what happens now; what we are up the line is connected to what we are now. If children are not temperamentally or physically suited to sports, or if they are in a sports environment that thwarts their success, there is the danger that key developmental issues will not be resolved positively and motivational desires will be unfulfilled.

I worry about the child who doesn't measure up to the ideals of his or her sport. How serious the mismatch can be without being harmful I can't say with any precision. It depends on the meaning the individual child attributes to sports. If it is just one among many things he or she does, if it is no big deal to the child, that's one thing. But if sports is a very important or *the* most important activity in a youngster's life, then the discrepancy between the ideals and expectations and the child's performance becomes a matter of concern. I'm not saying a child has to be the star of the team, but I know I worry about the kid who, for example, is only allowed to stand out in right field for the last couple of innings. And frankly, I also worry about the child who is mediocre on the field, about what effect sports is having on that child developmentally.

I have read and heard a great deal about how resilient children are. It is reassuring to hear about how tough kids are, how they get over things, and so on. Children *can* weather adversity, there's no doubt about that. But children are fragile too. They very much need our protection. They need our wisdom and our guidance. Of course, there are some lessons children need to learn about failure. With that said, however, it must be reiterated that at bottom the path to children's positive development is through confronting challenge successfully. Parents aren't all-powerful; they can't control everything in their children's lives. But that reality shouldn't stop parents from setting a goal to shoot for: to help their children get involved in situations, sports and otherwise, where they can take on manageable challenges. That is what is healthiest for children. That is what growing up is about ideally. I can imagine times when the best thing a parent can do is to caution a child against participating in organized sports and to help the child identify and serve his or her needs and desires in other ways. Parents don't always have to go along with anything their children want to do. They *do* always have to love their children and believe in them and want and work for the best for them. That means taking on the tough job of identifying the times when what the child wants contradicts what the child needs, and then doing something about it.

We want our children to grow up to have pride in themselves, to have a disposition toward curiosity and wonder, to be powerful, and to view the world as a meaningful place that can be understood and mastered. We want our children to be initiators, not reactors, in life, to chart their own course, or, as one author puts it, to be origins and not pawns in the world.[20] We want confident children, not fearful children. Sports and everything else in children's lives has to be judged on the basis of its effect on the dreams we have for our children and the dreams they have for themselves.

There is a prevailing sentiment in our culture these days that de-values parents and justifies parental aloofness. All the talk about "quality time" and the dangers of "smother love" has justified parents' distance from children and neutrality toward their endeavors. With children's lives becoming increasingly dominated by the school and peers and the popular culture, it seems to me the time has come for mothers and fathers to move closer to center stage. It is time to affirm the right and obligation of parents to involve themselves more directly with their children and to assert a steady influence on them. I don't mean dictating to children; that wouldn't work in any case. I do mean being authentic and honest with them, letting them know where you stand and what you stand for, and being a continuous and felt presence in their lives. At the very least, you should not defer to every other force that is shaping your children and should not feel compelled to endorse and support your child's whims and interests whatever they might be lest you be an "interfering parent."[21]

I believe what most compels Ken and Melissa Heise's investigation, and yours and mine, into the nature of sports and its effect on children is that it is one place where children play the growing up game, a game where the quality of their lives is on the line. We can talk about children succeeding and failing in the big football or basketball or soccer game and the consequences of that. But we need to remember that Ken and Melissa Heise, and all parents, are in a very big game themselves—as coaches of their children as they play the game of growing up. The consequences of winning and losing that game are monumental.

CHAPTER 3

Sports and Academics

In his letter to me, Ken Heise indicated that his wife, Melissa, worries that sports will interfere with their children's schoolwork. Of course she is not alone; virtually every parent—and I know this includes Ken—shares her concern. No matter how much parents may value a sports experience, they don't want their children involved in anything that will pull them down in their classes. What makes the connection between playing sports and academic success a particularly intriguing issue is the fact that many people hold just the exact opposite view from Melissa's. As they see it, not only doesn't participation in sports detract from schoolwork, it actually contributes to improving academic performance.

Conventional wisdom can be invoked to make a compelling case for both sides of the argument. On the negative side, there is the strongly embedded image of jocks who slough off in their schoolwork. There they are—we have all been around them—decked out in their hero jackets and stuffed into desks in the back of the classroom, smirking and joking around or, alternatively, frozen in apprehension or stunned by incomprehension. It is a widely held view that sports has the tendency to captivate children to the point that it shapes their attitudes, consumes their attention, and draws upon their energies, and does it in a way that is detrimental to their studies. The image is of kids going through the motions in school preoccupied by memories of the last game or fantasies about the next one. For these youngsters, school is chiefly—or even exclusively—a place to play ball, and that's not good.

But then again, there is the contrasting image of the all-around good kid, every parent's dream: good student, good athlete, good citizen, the whole package. There it is, right there in the list—good athlete—on equal standing with the other personal qualities we value so much. In this ideal, sports is an integral aspect of an exemplary life, a key, and very likely necessary, part of what makes up this young person. It seems certain that sports involvement is a factor that strongly contributes to the excellence, including academic excellence, of this youngster. Sports, it is believed, teaches youngsters to value accomplishment, set high goals, push hard, stick with it, and get things done, and that approach carries over to their schoolwork. Also there is the assumption that sports on someone's resume is a help academically because it gives this young person a leg up in getting admitted to a good college. Knowing that I was writing this book, several students sought me out to tell me that playing sports has helped them do better in their classes. They report that they achieve better grades during the season of their particular sport than during the off-season. Among the reasons they cite for this state of affairs are that sports helps them manage their time better, makes them more disciplined, gives them a reason to go to school, cuts the boredom, and just generally gives them a more positive attitude toward school.

So what are we to believe? Between these two conflicting conceptions of the connection between athletics and academics, where does the truth lie? Of course, one possibility is that even though these perceptions conflict, they do not contradict one another. It could be that both are valid to some extent, that sports distracts some students from their schoolwork and not others, and that for some reason people tend to focus exclusively on one group or the other. If that is the case, how can parents know which group their child will fall into? If we can't say that sports is invariably going to have one impact or the other on a particular youngster, can we at least generalize about the consequences of involvement in sports on children's orientation to their studies and success in school? Does one of these opposing views hold up better to scrutiny than the other? Perhaps I can shed some light on these questions. I have looked at the research evidence, probed what scholars and others have to offer on the subject, tapped my own experience, and thought about it. I will share what I found out and what I think. Then you will have to weigh the evidence and draw your own conclusions.

RESEARCH FINDINGS

What does the research say about the association between sports participation and academic success? Studies conducted to answer this question indicate that athletes as a group do have modestly higher grade point averages and greater aspirations than those who do not participate on varsity teams. Aspiration in these studies is most often measured by the desire of a youngster to go on to further education after high school.[1] As for the contribution of sports to academic accomplishment, evidence indicates that when sports is positively linked to academic performance it may be because of things that go along with the sports involvement rather than something inherent in the sports activity itself. Sport sociologist Jay Coakley highlights the kinds of relationships that are outgrowths of playing sports:

> After reviewing numerous studies on this topic, one finds that sport participation is positively associated with academic achievement and aspirations only when it somehow alters important relationships in a young person's life. When participation, for whatever reason, leads parents, friends, coaches, counselors, or teachers to take young people more seriously as human beings *and* as students, and give them more *academic* support and encouragement, participation will be associated with positive academic outcomes.[2]

Thus, improved academic performance could, for example, come out of a relationship that the athlete develops with a coach who takes the role of an academic confidant or advocate. A youngster might feel less pressure to present an image of academic competence to a coach than to a parent or teacher and therefore be more willing to share academic weaknesses and concerns and accept help. Another possibility is that sports is a highly valued endeavor in schools, and playing sports might lead to a more favorable view of a student among teachers. This could increase the chances of athletes getting the borderline grade called in their favor—for instance, when it is close and could be either a C+ or a B, the student-athlete gets the B.

All this is speculation, however. A major problem in interpreting the research on the connection between sports and academics is the difficulty in discerning clear cause-and-effect relationships. Virtually all the research has been in the form of correlational studies that compare groups of athletes and non-athletes. These investigations demonstrate how the groups differ from one another—and, indeed, that can be valuable information—but they leave open the question of *why* this difference exists. To illustrate, even if athletes as a group do get better grades than non-athletes, that still leaves the question of whether sports played any part in causing this difference. Did the youngsters learn something through sports, or did sports change them in some fashion, that led to greater success in school? Perhaps, but we also must think about whether the children who play sports have more of an achievement orientation and greater academic ability to begin with. Do athletes bring these qualities with them to sports rather than learn them on the field?

We need to assess family influences. Do families who encourage children to participate in sports also encourage them in academics as well? Might it be that what we are really measuring when we compare athletes' academic performance and aspiration levels to others' is the extent of family support? Might it also be that young people who have positive attitudes toward school tend to go out for the teams, whereas those who have less favorable attitudes stay away from sports programs? Do athletes take easier classes and thereby improve their grade-point averages? Also, we have to keep in mind that the group of athletes used for comparison purposes includes few if any of the students who are doing very poorly academically. Low-achieving students are probably not strongly encouraged to try out for sports, and in most schools poor grades result in being dropped from the team. By school policy, then, only passing students play sports and failing students are counted in the non-athlete group and bring down its average.

Often, research findings only tell us that there is a measurable difference between or among things without concern for the magnitude of the difference. We need to remember in those cases that the difference could be large, or it could be very small. If it is very small, we have to ask ourselves whether the difference matters in any practical way. We also have to assess whether the gain, large or small, is worth the time and energy expended to obtain it. Let's say that sports does tend to contribute positively to something we care about, attitude toward school, for example. We have to weigh that amount of improvement in attitude against all the time and effort that went into sports, all the practicing and games and thinking and talking about it and so on. On balance, was it all worth it? Also, was sports the only, or best, way to accomplish an improved attitude toward school? Was there some other, equally as good or even better, way to have obtained this good outcome? And, too, we have to weigh any positive outcomes of sports against all the not-so-positive outcomes of the endeavor: any negative impact sports had on social skills and orientations, on personality, on self-esteem, and so on. We may find that not-so-positive outcomes cancel out or outweigh the positive ones.

And what *didn't* happen that might have if the youngster hadn't been involved in sports? We need to ask how sports involvement compares with what could have been experienced or achieved if the child had been involved in some other activity? One way to measure the cost of something is to measure it against other things that could have been done instead. Call this the *opportunity cost*. The opportunity cost of playing sports is any other activity that the child could have engaged in instead: reading, learning to play a musical instrument, being with people other than the coaches and athletes, thinking about any other topic the child could have thought about if he or she had been thinking about sports, and so on.

In addition, it must be remembered that even though athletes on the average have slightly higher grades than non-athletes, it does not follow that to be an athlete is to do well in school. These are averages, numbers, not people. Individual cases will depart from what is on average so. In fact, a group with a relatively high average could include many who are not doing very well in their schoolwork. The presence of a few highly exceptional students, or the absence of any truly horrendous ones, can boost the average score for the group. Moreover, the nature of the group the athletes are compared to must be taken into account: How good are they? What if the non-athletes aren't particularly burning it up in school? In that case, we could have a situation in which athletes are simply relatively better than another group that isn't all that good themselves. There is some research evidence (and this certainly squares with my experience) that whatever the statistical averages might be, there are a good number of student-athletes who do not have positive attitudes about school. A study of 1000 male high school students revealed that half of those in varsity athletics had poor attitudes toward school and poor study habits.[3]

Finally, even if athletes on the average do better academically than non-athletes, that doesn't preclude the possibility that involvement in sports did in fact detract from their schoolwork. It could be that these youngsters would have done *even better* in their studies if they hadn't participated in athletics. That is to say, sports might have brought them down some academically, but they were so much better to begin with that they still came out on top of the non-athlete group in school performance.

A study of high school athletes, conducted by Herbert Marsh, was designed to get around the problems of correlational studies.[4] Marsh reports that there are indeed some positive effects of playing sports, with the largest being its favorable impact on the young person's social self-concept (the perception of one's social status and popularity). Marsh noted a small positive effect of sports involvement on academic self-concept (one's view of oneself as a student). Interestingly, however, his study did *not* show an improvement in *overall* self-concept. The Marsh study found that participation in sports leads to an increased commitment to school values and involvement with school. Marsh concluded that sports apparently adds to, rather than subtracts from, time, energy, and commitment to academic pursuits. As well, his investigation showed that sports has a small positive effect on each of the following: being in the academic track, good school attendance, taking academic and honors courses, taking science and math courses, and going on to higher education. However, as important as these positive outcomes may be in themselves, based on the Marsh findings it does not appear that they can be trusted to lead to improved academic *performance*, which he found unaffected by sports participation. The Marsh study did not find that sports participation improves grades, raises standardized test scores, or heightens occupational aspirations. On the other hand, Marsh found no significant negative effects of playing sports. He also concluded that the outcomes of playing sports are fairly consistent across race, class, and sex distinctions.

ASSESSING THE RESEARCH

What do I make of the research on sports participation and academic success? I don't see anything in the research that sends up a red flag indicating that sports is likely to be harmful to academic success, at least as these researchers define success, grade-point average and college aspirations. (I'll explore the usefulness of aspirations as a measure and offer another definition of academic success later in this chapter.) On the whole, athletes seem to do as well if not a bit better academically than their nonathlete counterparts. At the same time, what I have seen has squelched any enthusiasm I might have had for the idea that sports can be trusted to contribute to increased levels of academic accomplishment. Probably for most youngsters involvement in sports doesn't have an effect on grades one way or the other. This is not to say I don't hold out the possibility of sports turning a child on to school. My best estimate, however, is that there are significantly fewer of these children than many suppose, and I haven't yet seen any research supporting the popular claim that sports is likely to jumpstart a lackluster student.

What particularly strikes me are all the qualifiers that must be placed on the assertion that sports enhances academic achievement. Several things stand out in the research. First, it seems to show that sports doesn't help when it is the only form of extracurricular activity for a student. In light of this finding, one writer advises coupling school sports with leadership and service activities.[5] Second, there is evidence that sports doesn't do anything for low-ranking team members (end-of-the bench substitutes, fumblers and bumblers), or for participants in so-called minor sports, sports that don't get much attention in the school and community. Third, sports doesn't seem to do anything for grades and academic aspirations in schools where academics are emphasized and rewarded over and above sports performance.[6] This underscores the fact that not everyone has the same experience in sports: kids are different, schools and coaches and teams are different, and it is one thing to be the star halfback and something else to be the third-string tackle.

As for aspirations, we need to reflect on whether college aspirations are always good. We need to think more about how we might be pushing college on young people for whom it just isn't appropriate and making them feel they are failing us if they want to do something else. It is also important to distinguish aspiration from actual attainment. Someone can aspire to something and not achieve it. Although high academic aspirations are obviously important, they won't be realized if the young person lacks the necessary academic skills and orientations. And we must distinguish aspirations from expectations. I may aspire to something and yet deep down expect that I won't attain it, and that could hold me back. How hard are we going to charge after something we really don't feel in our hearts we deserve or think we are going to accomplish?

This distinction between aspiration and expectation is very important. I am convinced that what we actually get in our lives—you, me, children, all of us—is more than anything tied to our deepest personal expectations. Not what we want, not what we need, not even what we go after, as important as I acknowledge that to be. What we *expect* is in fact the biggest determinant of what we *get*. And I am not talking about what we tell ourselves or others we expect. I mean what we deep in our bones expect. As for kids, yes, I want to know what they aspire to, indeed that is important; but also tell me what they expect for themselves—that is even more important.

Where do children's expectations come from? In large part, they derive them from the expectations of them held by important people and forces in their world: teachers, friends, society (society expects certain things from children of "their kind"), religion, and—so important—parents. Children get the message from all these sources: *This is what we expect of you, and this is what you can expect of yourself. This is how life is going to work out for you.* Children pick up these messages beginning at a very young age, perhaps as young as a year or two. Children's brains don't mature until they are older—10 or 12 or so—and they aren't yet good with language, so young children receive and store these messages largely in a total, organic, kinesthetic way rather than as words and ideas. (Older children and adults absorb them in this way too, but it is more mixed in with concepts and articulate generalizations.) Children carry along these messages inside themselves, mostly in the form of pervasive, inner, physically felt sensations that hold the global meaning for them, *This is how things work out for me.*[7]

Moreover, children are observers of themselves from age 7 or so onward. They take note of what they do and how well things turn out for them, and these observations remain with them as memories and emotions and conclusions about what they can expect to accomplish. Children carry all this—the feelings, the messages, the observations—with them throughout childhood and into adult life, confirming it and elaborating on it as they go along. It is a constantly available inner reality that gives them direction and answers the question, *What's really going to happen to me?* By and large, both children and adults "keep their story going"—that is, probably without even realizing it, arrange their lives so that things work out just about as, underneath it all, they assume they will. Individuals are just about this successful, no more and no less; just about this happy, no more and no less; just about this loved, this acknowledged, this central, this influential, and so on.

What does all this mean for parents? It means that expectations matter a great, great deal. Watch closely what you expect of your child. To the degree you can, hold high expectations for your child, believe in your child, and, in your own way, consistently, frequently, let your child know that that is your posture toward him or her. To the extent you can, make sure your child is around people—teachers, coaches, others—who will expect a lot of your child. Going back to the discussion in the last chapter, do your best to put your child in situations where the results of your child's efforts will lead him or her to the feelings and thoughts that add up to, "When I give it my best, things turn out well for me." Last, when you sense your child is old enough, talk with him or her about the importance of holding high expectations of themself and combating anything inside or outside them that says, "This is your level; stay down there in that slot."

It intrigues me why so many people think sports has such a positive influence on academics when from what I have been able to discover the facts don't support this belief. Part of the answer seems to lie in the role the media plays in shaping our views about the effects of playing sports. I have in front of me a newspaper column originally published in the *Washington Post* entitled "True Jocks, With Brawn and Brains."[8] The author writes, "The myth of the Dumb Jock [is] an enduring conceit that many scholars say is not merely arrogant and hurtful but also conspicuously false." He notes that the high school athlete "typically outperforms his or her non-athletic peers in the classroom." He then goes on to cite the Marsh research discussed above, which he says discloses that sports participation appears to enhance self-image and school performance.

As reported earlier in this chapter, it is true that athletes as a group have a modestly higher grade-point average than non-athletes (although there was a long list of considerations and qualifications attached to that generalization). But as for this journalist's claim that the Marsh research discloses sports participation appears to enhance school performance, Marsh's study didn't show that at all. And as for sports enhancing self-image, because this writer does not specify what he means by self-image, readers are likely to assume that self-image refers to a youngster's overall or general view of himself or herself. Although the Marsh study found that sports somewhat increases social self-concept and academic self-concept (Marsh never used the term self-image), Marsh did not conclude that sports enhances overall self-concept. In fact, Marsh noted that an ever-so-slight *decrease* in overall self-concept results from playing sports.

People who read this piece on the editorial page aren't likely to go to the library and research the Marsh study to check out the writer's claims, and therefore are apt to be left with an incomplete picture and the perception that some things happen as a consequence of sports that don't. Did this writer intentionally mislead readers? My guess is no, he did not. People, journalists included, filter reality through their own experiences, values, and expectations, and without realizing they are doing so, distort it. There is nothing malicious in this. It is just that objectivity is tough to come by. If you have personally had a good time in sports and believe strongly that it is a good thing for children, and your child loves gymnastics, it is a short step from there to writing about sports making good things happen when the source you cite to support that contention doesn't really say that.

This example underscores how much of what we know—or think we know—comes to us through the media: television, newspapers and magazines, film, and the rest. I assume that most journalists, television commentators, and others who interpret the world for us, whether it is in the area of sports or some other, do it conscientiously and as honestly as they can. For that matter, so do coaches, athletes, parents of athletes, and anyone else who tells us about sports. But they each have assumptions and convictions that shape what they tell us, and we have to take that into account.

GRADE-POINT AVERAGE AND SPORTS PARTICIPATION

In 1986 the National Collegiate Athletic Association (NCAA) adopted Proposition 48, which required incoming freshman athletes to post a 2.0 grade-point average in at least eleven high school core courses and achieve a minimum combined score of 700 on the SAT or 18 on the ACT in order to be eligible for first-year scholarships and competition. Stricter standards along those same lines went into effect in 1995 and 1996, and it was at this point that the guidelines started to take a notable toll on athletes, particularly those from

African-American and low-income backgrounds. In 1997 the NCAA reported that 26 per cent of blacks identified as prospective major-college athletes failed to meet the standard of eligibility. This percentage had doubled from its status prior to the implementation of the tougher requirements. Although the failure rate of white athletes was much lower at 6.5 percent, that rate was three times what it had been prior to 1995. Athletes from low-income backgrounds were also hit hard by the new regulations; more than 22 percent failed to meet the standard compared to 9.8 percent two years earlier. The failure rate among athletes from upper-income families rose from 2 percent to 4.6 percent.[9]

These percentages for African-American and low-income athletes (and these are not altogether distinct groups since black athletes often come from low-income backgrounds) are a cause for concern. Although it could be that the raise in percentages since 1995 were to be expected as athletes adjusted to the new requirements—only time will tell. What is clear is that the eligibility regulations do have an effect on marginal students, pressing them to work harder on their school-work. (Or cheat—there have been persistent rumors of funny-business with the SAT and ACT exams of top-flight athletes in major sports.) However, even though some students increase their effort in their classes and prep harder for standardized tests in response to NCAA regulations and "no pass/no play" high school rules, I still am left with reservations about these get-the-grades-and-scores-or-else measures. First, among many student-athletes these regulations foster only a temporary concern for academics. The message to many youngsters is "attend to your academic 'illness' until the crisis passes, and then get back to business playing ball." This is similar to people who only attend to their health when they face a medical emergency and then revert to poor health habits; through it all, their fundamental posture toward their health remains unchanged. Also, I see a "minimums mentality" among students resulting from, for example, the requirement to maintain a C average to stay on the team. In the school's eyes it is setting a minimum requirement, hoping that students will rise above it. But from the students' perspective, they often interpret it as, "Here's your goal: a C average. Make sure you don't fall below this level." What is meant to be a minimum requirement becomes the student-athlete's highest goal.

As much as I value academics, I have serious misgivings about denying the right to a student to play on the school teams because of low grades or performance in class. The arguments for the practice are sincere and compelling: that academics comes first, that sports participation is a privilege, and that the threat of the loss of sports involvement can be used to improve schoolwork. Nevertheless, when you get down to the human level, it involves telling a young person who has been responsible and productive in one of the school's programs—presumably a program that the school considers to be of worth to students—that he or she is being excluded from it. I have problems with that. It takes away whatever benefit the child was getting from the sports activity. Moreover—and far more important as far as I am concerned—there is a fundamental cruelty involved in taking away something a child loves to do that is not negative or harmful to others. Even if using sports as a club to punish him brings him into line, that isn't enough to make it justified. Just because something is effective does not make it moral. For that matter, literally clubbing students might get them to attend to their studies, but that doesn't make it right.

In my view, if the child is in school, he or she ought to be able to participate in any of the school's programs as long as he accords himself well in that activity. That means if he is on the sports team and performs responsibly and to a reasonable standard of accomplishment he ought to be able to stay there, period. If there is a grade point average problem, then the problem is with his classes, not in sports, and ought to be handled there and not in sports. If the child is having a problem in, say, a math class, indeed it may be that sports is interfering with his performance in math. It is fair for the school to point out that fact to the child (as well as hear him out about why he thinks there is a problem, such as a poor teacher) and to relate how important math is and what he will have to do to improve in math and how the school will assist him in bringing about that improvement. But the choice of whether to drop sports ought to be with the child. If the child stays in sports and as a result flunks math, give him an F; if this class is required, don't let him graduate. Teach the child that he will experience the consequences of his choices and actions in every aspect of his life: what he gets out of sports aligns with what he does in sports, and what he gets out of math aligns with what he does in math.

I believe in concerned involvement and guidance, but not in controlling the child or doing things for him—especially after the child reaches 10 or 11 years and when it involves people outside the family. Schools mean well in trying to save the child from himself by removing him from the team against his will. Doing that, however, robs the child of the power of choice and the opportunity of taking responsibility for his conduct. In addition, there is the danger of unintended consequences: a child who waits around until the bottom drops out and someone punishes or saves him to bring him in line, or a bitter, resentful, defeated human being.

I don't accept the academics-comes-first argument. You've heard it:

"What kids have to understand is that their schoolwork comes first, then sports. They have to get their priorities straight." That sounds unimpeachable enough, but I don't like the idea of holding back on anything you commit yourself to doing in life, especially something you enjoy or find rewarding or that expresses who you are or develops you in important ways—and sports can be any and all of that. My view is that *everything* you do comes first. In this case, it is not classwork *or* sports, or classwork *over* sports; it is classwork *and* sports. If you do it, if you give your time and energy to it, whatever it is, do it 110 percent as they say in sports.

The PASS program I wrote about in the introduction doesn't tell young athletes to back off on sports in favor of their schoolwork. Instead, sports participation is *emphasized*, not de-emphasized or threatened. Their manner of engaging their sport is used as a metaphor and exemplar to guide youngsters' conduct in other areas of their lives, including and especially school. When you think about it, this is a very different approach from the one normally employed with kids who care about sports. The PASS program's message to young people is this: Go at your sport even harder than you are now, and at the same time bring your classwork up to that standard. Use your sport achievement as a measure of excellence to guide your work in your classes. Learn from what you do well and what gives you satisfaction in sports. Apply the attitudes, orientations, and skills that bring you success on the field to achieving greater success in the classroom. Quit living with a big contradiction in your life: being proud and self-reliant and goal-directed and accomplished in sports, and just the opposite in school. You are not going to be happy or feel good about yourself with that going on.

Whereas research has tended to focus on grades and college aspirations as measures of academic success, I believe I speak for the majority of parents when I say that we want our children to do more than just get good grades or aspire to college. We want them to develop their minds. We want them to be learning more than a collection of facts and isolated skills, regardless of what grade they get for doing it. We want them to learn that which will enable them to live the most honorable, satisfying, and productive lives possible. We want them working purposefully and hard to acquire the knowledge and capabilities that are the mark of an educated person in this society. We want them to value learning and intellectual growth. We want them to be curious and explore the world and to think creatively about it. We want them to give meaning to what they learn. We want them to read widely about important things and think about what they read. We want them to become independent learners, people who know how to learn new things—a vitally important capability in this time of rapid change. These are criteria for measuring academic success that go beyond grade-point averages and simply whether a youngster wants to continue in school.

As a teacher, I want to contribute to youngsters becoming what I have come to call *true students*. True students are *self-surpassing* students. As individuals, they go to school intent on going beyond their current level of learning and accomplishment in their classes. True students walk into the classroom door intending to get something positive done. They don't just fall into a seat and wait to see what comes up. They don't just respond to whatever happens to catch their attention or do only what they are compelled to do by the teacher. True students are questers. They search for knowledge, self-understanding, and greater competence. True students are students in the sense that they are *studying* something. Many students are taking and passing classes and accumulating a good grade-point average, perhaps even getting on the honor roll, and still they aren't actively studying anything.

Whether or not a child is a true student matters vitally, because being a true student is the way for a young person to get the most out of school. It is the way to learn the most and to grow the most as a person. It hones positive qualities and values such as a respect and desire for knowledge, a commitment to one's own development as a person, and the desire to express oneself in the world. Being a true student is the best way to acquire true knowledge. True knowledge occurs when you *really* know something rather than just have a fact on hand for the hour of the test. To really know something, you have to *appropriate* it, not just receive it. You don't really learn something by passively listening to someone tell you about it or simply doing the job put in front of you. You really learn it by having the goal of learning it, and then taking on the responsibility of learning it, and then wrestling with the challenge until you get it done. To really know something you have to think about it, give it meaning, relate it to other things, make sense of how knowing this makes you different from the way you were before, and decide what you are going to do with this new knowledge or skill or attitude or area of interest. In the process of really learning something you can listen to a teacher's lecture or complete a teacher's assignment, but the meaning these activities have for you is that they are instrumental in getting you where you are taking yourself.

True students operate in this way. However, to approach school in this fashion takes self-conscious, thoughtful engagement with one's schoolwork and a great deal of time and energy. And here's the point: I don't see sports involvement leading students in this direction, toward being true students. I have seen instances in which sports served to encourage students to take school more seriously and get better grades, and yes, that is important. But I have observed and taught very few athletes whom I considered to be true students. I worry that there are aspects of the sports experience for young people who get deeply involved in it that discourage, or at least do not encourage, becoming true students. There have been wonderful exceptions to be sure, but both at the high school and the university levels, the majority of student-athletes I have taught and observed appeared to be better typed as task-completers than true students. It is as if they see school as a hoop to jump through, and they diligently and soberly do just that. I include in this characterization most all of the young people who are held up to be exemplary student-athletes. They do the work, it's solid even if it doesn't sparkle, many teachers, even though they don't feel quite right about it, wind up giving them a B+ or an A. The young people I have in mind are polite, deferential (almost too much sometimes), and at the same time a bit mechanical and not quite "there."

It is understandable that it is this way. Sports are fun and exciting. Although school is important and potentially growth-producing and satisfying, I wouldn't use fun and exciting to describe very much of it. In addition, as we discussed in the last chapter, sports is often an arena for the resolution of vital personal issues. With so much getting done besides playing ball, it makes sense that sports would capture children's attention and contribute to a view of schoolwork as something to get out of the way so they can get to the real action. It should be no wonder, then, that children don't keep sports in its proper place in their lives. In particular, it shouldn't surprise us given how frequently schools put sports virtually on a par with academics in what they emphasize and value. (I will delve into this issue in detail in Chapter 5.)

The one serious concern I have in this entire sports-and-academics area based on my experience in education is that more than a few children will become worse *students* because of sports. This could be the case even (and this is where it can get complicated) in instances when grades are high, or going up, as the result of a plodding, dutiful, but uninspired approach to schoolwork that is often rewarded with good grades. What parents most need to watch out for, in my view, is the possibility that sports will affect children's priorities and turn them off—or prevent them from turning on—to the life of the mind.

CHAPTER 4

Does Sports Build Character?

Ken Heise's letter to me spoke of his belief that sports builds character in children. He's not alone in this belief; it is a widely held view. The character-building dimension of sports is one of the central arguments sports advocates use to urge children's involvement in sports. In Chapter 1, I quoted Judy Oppenheimer on her belief that football had taught her son lessons about courage and hard work and putting himself on the line. I have in front of me a book that is equally unequivocal: "Sports *does* build character." [Emphasis in the original.] The author goes on to say, "Sports preparation is life preparation. It *does* help a child to overcome adversity, deal with pressure and act responsibly within the community."[1] As I did with other assertions of this sort, I looked for elaboration or documentation that would justify this contention, but I didn't find any. This got me thinking more about the extent to which some of the ideas we have about sports are untested articles of faith, and it reinforced my desire to check out for myself the support for these sorts of claims.

As I listen to people talk about character and read about it, I am struck by the wide range of qualities encompassed within that term, including such traits as honesty, self-discipline, sportsmanship, emotional stability, assertiveness, independence, and good citizenship. Some of the sports research I have reviewed included within the definition of character such things as academic achievement and social skills. Such an inclusive definition makes any precise discussion impossible.

I will list and briefly comment on four personal characteristics that, to me, make up character. Knowing how I see character will give you a better understanding of the way I approach this issue, as well as make my conclusions and recommendations clearer to you. Also, I hope that by setting out my view of character you will be encouraged to think more about the directions in which you want to see your children's character develop, and why.

In my view, good character comprises four traits: responsibility, integrity, decency, and independence. To the degree that someone has these four qualities, I consider this person to have good character.

1. *Responsibility*. This person is responsible to the situations and requirements in his or her life. He or she is someone whom you can trust to take on the job that needs to be done and stay with it. A responsible person is self-disciplined and persistent. This is someone who works hard, with care, and has high standards.

A second sense of responsibility is that this person owns his or her status in life. This person accepts responsibility for himself or herself and doesn't offer excuses or put responsibility on someone or something else for his or her level of happiness, satisfaction, and accomplishment.

A third sense in which people are responsible is that they take responsibility for their own development as a person. Each seeks to become the best possible version of who he or she is as a unique human being, and to express that uniqueness in all aspects of life.

2. *Integrity*. This person lives according to personal values. There is a consistency between this individual's deepest convictions and his or her conduct in the world. A responsible person has a commitment to live honorably.

3. *Decency*. This person is directed by a firm sense of what is just and fair. Decent people are not simply driven by what is possible, pleasant, or to their own advantage. They respect the rights and dignity of others. They are compassionate and generous. They are loyal. Decent people don't abandon people and projects and obligations.

4. *Independence*. This person is not the tool of someone else. Independent people think for themselves; they don't just go along with the crowd.

Notice that in this list of character traits I include a number of opposites. For example, a person with character in my eyes is someone who is oriented toward himself—self-expressive, committed to his own well-being—and at the same time compassionate and respectful and generous to others. He is independent and can also be counted on to uphold his responsibilities to his family, his friends, and his group. In fact, a good way to see character is as the integration of a number of contrasting qualities into a harmonious and complementary whole.

I believe a person should bring his character to sports. He should play sports in the same way he should engage in all other activities. He should not view himself, or allow himself to be defined by others, as the embodiment of a role or a cog in a system, in sports or anywhere else. A person of character is a good sportsman. He plays hard and fair, with respect for his opponent, and with grace and dignity. Not only is sports a place to live out his character, it is also—like every other context in his life—a setting in which to *develop* his character.

SPORTS AND MORAL DEVELOPMENT

A major focus in the research on character has been on moral development. The assumption behind these studies is that just as people develop physically, mentally, and socially, so too do they develop morally. Morality has to do with matters of rightness and wrongness, goodness and badness, fairness and unfairness, justice and injustice. The question for us, of course, is what effect sports has on the moral orientation and conduct of children.

The details of the moral development theory undergirding this research need not concern us in this context.[2] Basically they focus on how individuals justify moral choices and behaviors. The higher stages of moral reasoning involve abstract, complex, and inclusive rationales for moral stances. As the theory has it, moral development is encouraged when an individual interacts with people who are at higher moral stages than his own and when higher forms of moral thought infuse a setting. In other words, morally we tend to become like the people we associate with and the places we frequent.

In recent years, some theorists have begun to focus less on an individual's development toward the formation of abstract principles of justice. Instead they have emphasized the ways people deal with one another in social situations. Many writers who reflect this relational orientation assert that the focus on abstractions misses the reality of most of the moral issues people face in their lives. Rather than focus on an individual's formation of ideas about morality, these writers emphasize the development of such attributes as helping, sharing, and caring for others. They explore the ways people relate to one another and resolve interpersonal conflicts. They place value on the processes of negotiation among interdependent parties and keeping stress and animosity in relationships to a minimum.[3]

What the relational perspective on moral development comes down to is a concern for the way we treat one another. It leads researchers to investigate such questions as whether in a particular group there is equal access to information and whether everyone who is affected by some matter is included and taken into account and given a voice. Is there unforced consensus through noncontaminated discussions, and does it reflect the peculiarities of the parties involved? Two theorists, Brenda Bredemeier and David Shields, reflect this relational orientation when they write, "Moral development refers to the evolving maturity of a person's grasp of the interpersonal rights and responsibilities that characterize social life."[4]

How does sports affect the morality of participants? Bredemeier and Shields propose that sports often promotes what they call *game reasoning*: "Sport elicits a transformation of moral reasoning such that egocentrism, typically the hallmark of immature morality, becomes a valued and acceptable principle of organizing the moral exchange."[5] That is to say, sports legitimizes regression to a lower level of morality. If they are right, what effect will that have on participants? Will this game-reasoning orientation remain limited to sport, or will it spill over into other parts of life? Even though research evidence indicates that high school athletes' moral reasoning levels don't differ from non-athletes', there is also data indicating that college athletes have lower moral reasoning levels than their non-athlete counterparts.[6] Should we take this to mean that a game mentality takes hold and starts to become a general moral orientation as athletes get older? Or is it that those who are at lower moral stages are more drawn to, or more successful in, college sports? At this point we can only speculate.

We do live in a society that would seem to promote the transfer of game reasoning to other areas of life. Sports images and metaphors are everywhere in business and politics: full court presses, horse races, knock-out punches, home runs, team spirit, and all the rest. Parents will have to watch how much sports encourages a philosophy that rationalizes winning at any cost, cheating, and aggression to get what you want as long as you can get away with it. In the rest of life there aren't the restraints sports provides—the rules and referees that operate as a check against this orientation. To be sure, there are laws and police. Nevertheless, society depends greatly on a shared sense of morality among its citizenry. The truth of the matter is that in society you can trip or block someone and most often there is no one to blow the whistle and call a foul on you. It can be a tough road for a society if its members must be on guard for game reasoning in one another.

Moral development researchers tend to equate egoism with immorality. My own view is that if a sport teaches your child to look out for his or her own interests, that isn't all bad. In this life, there are more than a few occasions when if you don't take care of your needs no one else will. That may not be the best of all worlds, and we could spend our time bemoaning that fact. However, I think you are better off if you learn how to play the game that is on the table, to use a sports metaphor. Otherwise, you may be taking everyone else's needs into account while they are busily getting theirs and leaving you with the short end of the stick. If a child learned from sports to put himself first, and actually developed that capability, I wouldn't be upset, that's the truth of it.

Moreover, egoism—a concern for one's self, self-centeredness—and exploitation of others don't have to go together. And I don't equate subordination or sacrifice of one's own interests with morality. If a sport emphasized only the interests of the team or the coach or the cause over my child's, I would give serious thought before encouraging my child to participate.

There is some evidence that sports often involves a trade-off among good things: that is, when traits such as independence and perseverance are emphasized in a sports setting, qualities such as cooperation, sharing, helping, empathy, and altruism may be undermined, and vice versa.[7] Research also has shown that even if athletes do learn positive social behaviors on the athletic field, very often they don't carry them over to other areas of life. This squares with my own experience. Often an athlete will be responsible and cooperative and achievement-oriented on the field and quite the opposite in the classroom and other contexts.

Sport sociologist Jay Coakley speculates that although the typical sports experience may produce negative outcomes, a carefully organized experience would be helpful. He points out, for example, that the martial art of tae kwon do teaches a philosophy of nonviolence, respect of one's self and others, the importance of fitness and control over self, confidence in one's physical skills, and a sense of responsibility.[8] Coakley thinks other sports could also explicitly teach such attributes. I suggest you think about martial arts training for your children—tae kwon do, aikido, or tai chi. All are ways of being in the world and not just about breaking boards or someone's nose.

Sports and morality isn't a simple picture because even as sports accepts a game morality, a code of sportsmanship pervades athletics. In sports, a concept of fair play runs counter to the "anything I can get away with" outlook. Hatchet men are criticized by the sports community, and the most honored athletes tend to be those who play by the rules.

What is certain is that children model themselves after those with whom they associate and situations shape the way they look at things—in the scholarly literature the process is called *social learning*. Ask yourself: *What kind of moral beings are the coaches and teammates of my child? Are they good, decent people? Are*

*these the moral examples I want my child to be around? Would I
want my child to be like them? What are the ideas about right and
wrong in this sports context? Would I want my child to use them to
guide his life on the playing field and in the other areas of his life?*
See what answers you reach.

COMPETITION AND COOPERATION

Competition does not fare well in the research. One study, for
example, reports data suggesting that when competition is allowed to
dominate the interpersonal relationships in children's sports, its
potential for facilitating the development of positive social behavior
is entirely lost.[9] This study and others like it might lead us to the
conclusion that all competition is bad. It isn't as far as I am concerned. I think competitiveness in its best form is a prosocial behavior. Beyond that, given the nature of life in this society I consider it
to be a necessary skill to possess.

The research defines competition as just one thing. But it isn't; it
comes in various forms. Competition is not the same in every instance. There are cases of cut-throat competition where anything
goes, and indeed that usually is a negative occurrence. But I have also
witnessed and participated in competition that was satisfying and
enhancing to everyone involved. Participants in a competition can
respect and honor one another and encourage one another to their
best efforts and most rewarding experiences. A very formative experience for me came many years ago when I attended the 1976 Olympics in Montreal and observed both the intense competition and
intense closeness of the athletes. It was beautiful to behold and in
such contrast to the us-against-them, winning-is-everything hype of
the television coverage at that time. I saw athletes who lost, in the
sense that they came in second or third or last. But what showed
through clearly along with these athletes' disappointment was their
joy of running in a race in the best physical condition of their life and
giving their all in communion (yes, competition can be a communal
experience) with fellow athletes. Every time I hear competition denigrated, I recall that time in Montreal.

It is not that I think competition is always healthy, but I also don't
indiscriminately reject competition as some vocal critics of sports
(and American life in general) are doing these days. Unlike some, I
don't see competition as necessarily conflicting with cooperation.
And I don't see cooperation as the inherently better, higher, more
acceptable process. "Cooperation is good; competition is bad"—that
is the message I am frequently getting these days. It sounds good and
it plays well—being for cooperation and against competition is a

fashionable and easy argument to make. But if you look at life as it is actually lived, it becomes clear that often competition is appropriate.

Consider, for example, the life of a teenager. There is competition all over the place—in school, in sports and recreation, socially, everywhere. A young person who either doesn't know how to compete or backs down in the face of competition is in trouble. I especially worry about those who most need to stand up and compete for their rightful place in the world—I am talking about the poor and neglected and abused in our society. They are too often the very ones who haven't learned to compete or shrink from doing it. These children had better learn to compete or they will remain on the periphery, trying to make do with the scraps they are able to gather for themselves or that have been tossed their way. If sports can teach kids to be competitive in a decent and honorable way, I am all for it.

We should be careful also not to take it for granted that a young person involved in a sport that we characterize as competitive is in fact competitive in that sport. I have seen many athletes playing a competitive sport who as a matter of fact were not very competitive in that situation. Some athletes hold themselves back because they are not competitive enough to take the most advantage of their ability.

Even though it would be useful, we haven't broken down and analyzed competition as we have, say, the golf swing. It would be useful if we could determine precisely what constitutes competition in its most positive form, and then figure out how to teach it to people who need to improve on it. It could be that one reason sports has not done more to break down competition into its elements and teach them to athletes is the widespread idea in sports that competitiveness is like grace, something one simply has or doesn't have, an inborn trait that can be manifested to a greater or lesser degree. From that frame of reference, competitiveness can't really be *taught*. All the coach can do is put players in a context in which the ones who "have it" can reveal that fact, and select them for the team and starting positions and continually exhort them and the other players to be more and more competitive.

As for cooperation, we need to question closely what people mean when they say they are for cooperation. Cooperation can be personally satisfying, as well as productive and socially beneficial. Currently, much of scientific discovery and business activity is a cooperative undertaking. But on the other hand, the Nazis cooperated very nicely to exterminate other human beings. I can personally attest to the fact that some of the most inane activities and useless outcomes imaginable are undertaken and achieved by committees operating in cooperative fashion. Slaves were urged to cooperate—as are prison road gangs.

The term *collaboration* more accurately defines the form of shared enterprise that I most value. Collaboration happens when people who know who they are, what they believe in, and what they seek to accomplish choose—voluntarily choose—to join others because it is the most effective and personally rewarding way to attain their goals. At their freest and at their best, human beings collaborate with one another. Some of what is applauded as teamwork in sports looks to me like the mindless activity of a sled team under the direction of a driver (coach). But in other instances I see players collaborating in beautiful ways. The point is, when I hear talk about teamwork, I want to hear more about it. Are the athletes drones in a beehive merely doing their jobs, or are they learning to collaborate in the way that men and women do at their best?

SPORTS AND CONFORMITY

I have heard it said that sports tends to produce malleable, conforming people. Some contend that sports inhibits the development of compassion and concern for social issues, social justice, and human rights. Some claim that it deadens political awareness and encourages compliance with established authority. Some regard sports as promoting political conservatism, which they see as a bad thing.

Studies do show athletes measuring higher on personal and political conservatism and lower on political awareness than their counterparts who are not involved in sports.[10] It is true that by and large, the sport culture has not been on the forefront of social change. Although one can think of a good number of exceptions to that generalization—for example, the protests at the 1968 Mexico City Olympics, and the career of the late Arthur Ashe. Perhaps people drawn to sports are not the most politically aware or concerned, or the most autonomous, individuals in the first place. People getting into sports know they are going to be taking orders and fitting into a tight system, and it could be that people who highly value their independence and autonomy try to stay clear of such a situation. With that said, however, there does seem to be enough of an issue here to warrant keeping your eye on whether the sports experience is to any degree cutting your child off from social and political concerns—making such issues seem unimportant, beside the point, or removed from his or her life—or fostering an antagonism toward social change.

DOES SPORTS KEEP KIDS OUT OF TROUBLE?

As for the widely held view that sports keeps kids out of trouble, no evidence in the material I have reviewed has indicated that there is anything about sports that systematically discourages bad behavior. On the other hand, studies haven't found higher rates of deviant conduct among athletes than non-athletes, and this is true for both males and females and those from all racial and social class backgrounds.[11] This should ease any worry that sports might be a breeding ground for crime, trouble-making, or social pathology. From what I can tell, an athlete is no more or less likely to mess up than anyone else.

SPORTS AND PERSONAL AUTONOMY

Sports is often credited with producing autonomous, independent people. My investigations and reflection tell me that the idea that sports produces self-directed people in a true sense is much overrated. We see kids out on the field apparently acting effectively on their own.   But we have to remember that most sports situations are top-down, hierarchical arrangements, with the coach in autocratic control and making virtually all the important decisions. Usually the coach sets up the schedule, picks the team, decides who starts and who substitutes, and calls the individual plays. Most athletes only take on responsibility for making tactical decisions—ways of achieving a game strategy decided on by a coach. Most organized sports emphasize obedience to the coach and learning to follow orders and taking on the role one is assigned. Effectively carrying out one's assignment should not be equated with achieving personal independence or self-determination. In fact, it may get in the way of true independence.

There have been many instances of athletes finding it difficult to set their own goals and priorities and chart their own course when they are outside the highly structured world of athletics. It could be that more than anything sports is teaching your child to do unquestioningly what he is told. This has its upside; there are times when it is appropriate to do what has been set out for you. But it has its downside too, if it gets in the way of learning how to set out good things to do for yourself and learning how not to be dependent on other people doing it for you all the time. I worry about the autocratic nature of so many sports settings, where the ideal is to follow orders no matter what. What kind of people does this circumstance foster?

SPORTS AND PROSOCIAL QUALITIES

Do athletes develop prosocial qualities from sports? I don't see it particularly, although I am open to be shown that they do. There is a

United Way-type community service orientation associated with professional athletes, although how much of that is team-encouraged public relations I don't know. In her book, *Dreams of Glory*, Judy Oppenheimer recounts how the high school football players on her son's team volunteered to protect women against a man who had been wandering down the street hitting women over the head. "Our heroes, our protectors," thought Oppenheimer, who was certain that football had been in large part responsible for the players' actions.[12] Oppenheimer writes of a toughness that came out of the football experience that she believes contributed to the social-protector role these athletes adopted. Of course, what she sees as an outgrowth of increased toughness may also have been to some degree a case of the boys venting in a socially approved way the aggressiveness that had been pumped up by their football experience—which may be positive in itself if the boys had learned to distinguish positive and negative ways to release aggression in football. In any case, Oppenheimer notes proudly, "They had struggled for three months to achieve that supreme state of grace in which you truly believed you were the toughest SOB coming down Rockville Pike."[13]   I'm not sure that one has to become the "toughest SOB coming down Rockville Pike," but I do agree that toughness, hardness, can be a positive attribute and can contribute to both social and personal betterment. Oppenheimer may well have a point.

SPORTS AND PERSONAL DEDICATION

It is remarkable how much time and effort some youngsters put into athletics: hours and hours of practice and games, attending clinics, reading and talking about their sport, watching others play to see what can be learned, and so on. The commitment and personal connection to sports that we see in athletes is laudable when contrasted with the relative indifference so many young people—and adults, for that matter—show toward just about everything. Sports promotes intense engagement and extraordinary perseverance among many of its participants. Often sports is the only force in a child's life that does promote that. The sports culture holds up the standard of *really* doing something rather than merely doing it, a standard that appears to be increasingly absent in the larger culture. Sports should be ap- plauded for that at a time when so many people do some of this and a little of that and nothing matters to them all that much.

With that said, however, we still need to be careful in our admira- tion of the dedication an athlete shows to his sport. It *may* be that children caught up in sports are learning what it takes to be successful and what it is like to invest oneself completely in an endeavor and experience the rewards that result. Sports dedication, persistence, and grit *may* transfer to other aspects of the athlete's life. But don't count on it. Unfortunately, sports dedication often doesn't carry over to other involvements. Many athletes learn to be dedicated *in sports*, and that's it. As well, we must be careful not to automatically equate dedication to a sport with virtue, or even positive results. The commitment to sports that we see may in fact be an obsession or compulsion, or an indication of personal incompleteness or immaturity.

Also, no matter how much you dedicate yourself to something, it may simply not be in you to be successful or to achieve satisfaction or personal growth in that activity. For some kids, working to develop basketball skills is like a fly bouncing up against a window over and over again. The most significant outcome for these youngsters will be, figuratively—or even literally—a headache. There are times when the best thing a child can do is quit the team and put his energies into something else. In fact, doing that may be a greatest victory this child can achieve in athletics. Putting a stop to dead-end activities—call it quitting if you'd like—is a valuable and necessary part of anyone's personal repertoire. It shouldn't be denigrated by calling up the slogans about always finishing what you start, sticking with it, not letting others down, and so forth. "Quitters never win and winners never quit" sounds good but isn't true.

WHY THE FAITH IN SPORTS' CHARACTER-BUILDING QUALITIES?

As when we examined the supposed connection between sports and improved academic performance, the more I looked into it the more intrigued I became about why people seem to be so firmly convinced that sports develops character. As far as I can tell, it is a dubious proposition. It seems that sports is hit and miss: helpful for some kids and not for others. For most kids, it seems, sports doesn't have a major effect on character one way or the other. Why, then, has the character-building property of sports become virtually an article of faith, to the point that people who talk and write about sports don't see any need to support their affirmations?

Again I think Jay Coakley is helpful as he lists three possible reasons for this phenomenon.[14] First, sports attracts and selects people with certain characteristics. For example, those with low confidence usually don't try out for the teams or are cut if they do try out. So it isn't that sports builds confidence; the athletes bring it with them. Coakley points out that if the data showed athletes were stronger or faster or more coordinated, we wouldn't automatically assume that sports made them that way. The sports experience could actually cut confidence down a bit and the athletes could still be relatively more confident than non-athletes because they started out so much higher.

Coakley's second point is that sports uses visible and top-level athletes as examples of the good things sports does for participants. Thus, we are making judgments from a biased sample; focusing on success cases and ignoring the rest doesn't give you the total picture. It is like taking a sample of Ph.D.s, physicians, and lawyers to characterize the success of the public school system, says Coakley.

The third reason Coakley offers for what appears to be the overestimation of sports' character-building potential is that sports events evoke visibly challenging situations. When we see athletes confronting these challenges successfully, we tend to assume they must have stronger character than the rest of us and that sports made them that way. However, it could be that spectators are seeing these young people demonstrate qualities they have had all along—for that matter, qualities the spectators may well possess themselves—qualities the athletes haven't had the chance to show in other contexts. Says Coakley, "What probably happens is that sport gives adults, especially parents, opportunities to see young people display traits that have developed over a number of years and across a variety of different experiences."[15]

To Coakley's three reasons, I'll add a fourth. Simply put, one reason that we think athletics develops character is because so many athletes and coaches *say* it does, and they are obviously sincere. However, in my research over the years, I have learned to bring what I hope is a healthy skepticism to assessing self-reports. The skepticism comes from my realization that people's experiences tend to conform to the way things are defined for them, and that people tend to believe in what they do, whatever it is.

I'll explain. First, there is the propensity of many people to go along with the prevailing view of something. The word comes down to them, it is part of the mythology of sports, a piece of conventional wisdom, that sports builds character. This becomes the context for them; they fit their experience into this context, use this context to give their experience meaning. People like to have things make sense. They don't like *dissonance*, a situation or condition where everything isn't nicely integrated, where this fact doesn't agree with that one, or this experience doesn't square with that assumption. Moreover, it creates discomfort to contradict what others believe. Other people don't like that and let you know. Alternatively, it feels good to be right, on the right side, inside, with those in the know. The result is that people pay attention to evidence that supports the character-developing thesis about sports, and they ignore the evidence that doesn't fit it.

Along with the tendency to accept "the way things are," people tend to believe in what they do, whatever it happens to be. It is clear that sports—for reasons we have already discussed—can draw participants deeply into the activity. And of course coaches, sportswriters, some athletes, and others make a living from sports. Whatever takes up a great deal of our time and energy and gets linked to our identity and gives us status or puts food on the table comes to be something we are likely to believe in quite fervently. Add the fact that even though there are going to be some who dropped out of the activity and who harbor negative views about it, by and large they aren't the ones we will hear from. Dropping out of sports has negative connotations—a quitter, couldn't hack it, not man enough, let the team down, and the like. Unless we are particularly secure in ourselves (and how many young people are?) this is something we don't announce to the world. Put all this together and what we get is a preponderance of heartfelt testimonials for the character-building merits of sports.

CONCLUSION

I have concluded that no matter how one wants to define character, athletes very likely have no more of it than members of any other group. Some athletes are wonderful people, some are out-and-out thugs, and most of them are average folks. I have heard it said that sports reveals character. I would qualify that contention and say that sports reveals *athletic* character, the person's character on the field of competition. The athlete might be very different somewhere, or everywhere, else.

Does the sports experience in any systematic way make kids more or less virtuous? Researcher Roger Rees and his colleagues note that empirical studies exploring whether sports makes someone a better person show that sports has either no effect or a slightly negative effect, results they say challenge the sports-build-character myth.[16] After studying and thinking about this myself, I have concluded that the most accurate thing one can say about sports is that it teaches and reinforces a particular way of thinking and being that differs from one athletic setting to another. It appears that for most kids sports has no significant impact one way or the other on what kind of people they become, and that when it does have an effect, the effect depends on both the nature of the child and the nature of the situation. Sports can have a negative effect on a child's character—envy of one's teammates, hostility toward opponents, cheating—especially in boys' sports. But at the same time—and these are positive possibilities Rees and his colleagues seem to underestimate—playing sports can lead to a commitment to fair play and healthy cooperation, and can help young people become more self-directed and responsible. However, here again, these positive attributes often remain sports-specific. Many athletes who are self-directed and responsible on the field are far from that in other areas of their lives. Although we need to recognize that reality, we should not let it obscure the young people whose character has been improved by their involvement in sports. Amid all the numbers and generalizations, let's not overlook them, even as we acknowledge that they are not typical.

CHAPTER 5

Why Is Sports So Central in Schools?

Until I did the research for this book I hadn't realized that schools in other parts of the world do not get involved in sports as extensively as schools in the United States. In most countries, organized sports for adolescents and young adults are tied to community-based athletic clubs.[1] We need to ask what possible positive or negative effects for children might stem from the close link between school and sports so prevalent in this country.

The message our schools send to students goes something like this: "We take sports seriously and we think you ought to, and we have a lot of teams, and if you don't get on one or more of them, well, that's all right with us, *but* . . ." The result is that most students feel pressure to decide what they are going to do about the school's sports programs. They must decide which ones they are going to try out for, and if they don't participate in sports, they feel compelled to justify it to themselves and the school and other students. Parents must realize that what they do about sports is no small matter for students in our schools, and increasingly this is true for girls as well as boys. I am hard-pressed to think of any other part of American life in which sports is such a big deal that it can essentially define who one is. I can offer some possible reasons for the centrality of sports in schools. I hope this discussion encourages you to think more about the beliefs, values, pressures, and rewards related to sports that children confront every day in schools.

REASONS FOR SPORTS' PROMINENCE IN SCHOOLS

To begin, *tradition* is one important reason for the prominence of sports in schools. Simply put, one of the reasons we do anything in a certain way—sports or anything else—is because that is the way we have done it before. Human beings have a tendency to stay with what they have been doing, and that is true regardless of how well or how poorly it is working for them. In that sense, the past controls us. Past practices come to be viewed not as an arbitrary selection from alternatives, but instead as the natural way to proceed—legitimate, appropriate, inherent in the scheme of things. The truth is that schools don't have to be in the sports business at all; they could leave that to someone else. But it is difficult for people who have known nothing else but the big game between Jefferson High and Lincoln High and the Homecoming Dance to realize that.

Another reason for their stress on sports is that schools are committed to the idea of a well-rounded person and sincerely believe that sports contributes to well-roundedness. Schools do not emphasize specialization. In sports terms, they believe in developing good utility players, people who can play all the positions. Students take math *and* science *and* social studies *and* English *and* physical education *and* art *and* music . . . *and* students are expected to get involved in extracurricular programs. A person can become a success in life by doing one thing well (plumbing or carpentry or selling insurance or flying an airplane) and by being responsible to one person they love and a few friends. You can do that in life, but not in school.

The fact that schools have taken on an increasingly broad responsibility over the course of the twentieth century gives impetus to athletics in schools. Besides the intellectual growth of their students, schools seek to produce good citizens. They also see themselves as job trainers, preparing students for entry into the economy. Schools promote the personal—in contrast to academic—development of students and attend to the full range of their physical and mental well-being. As other elements in the society (the family, the church, and the neighborhood) seem to indicate they won't or can't take on the task, schools have heightened their efforts in the areas of morality. Sports is assumed to contribute positively to all those areas. Clearly, if schools focused solely on academics, sports would not be as prominent in schools as they are.

Another reason for the high priority of sports in schools is that schools believe they see positive academic outcomes resulting from participation in sports. It is assumed that participating in sports contributes to greater interest in the school and better attitudes toward the school, including its academic programs. There is an assumption that success on the field can lead to heightened self-esteem and confidence and better work habits, and that this will spill over into the classroom. There is a belief that sports can lead to greater attention and support being given to a young person's academic performance by parents and teachers. Sports is seen as a motivator: having to keep their grades up to play sports, it is believed, compels students to attend to their schoolwork, and sports holds some kids in school who otherwise would not attend regularly or would drop out. As we have already discussed, these assumptions about the positive academic consequences attributable to sports are open to question, but that is beside the point here. What counts is that schools believe these things are true.

Universities and colleges influence schools to emphasize sports programs. The perception is that university and college admissions officers frown on academic drudges. They prefer students who have taken part in school and community activities. The result is that secondary schools feel pushed to provide opportunities for students to construct résumés to impress colleges and universities—student government, this club and that club, this sport and that one. Students, encouraged by their families, let it be known they need these opportunities. After all, they don't want colleges to think they sit in the library studying all the time; that wouldn't look good. Sports is also seen as the ticket to a college scholarship for some youngsters, and schools would feel guilty if they closed that door by not offering sports programs.

Also, school involves two generations living together in the same space. Generations rub each other the wrong way in any case, and that problem is compounded when one group is compelled to be there and is required to do whatever the other group tells it to do. When it comes down to it, most of the time teaching involves getting someone of a different generation to do something he or she would just as soon not do. In contrast, sports is something the kids actually *want* to do. What a relief for the adults!

Sports eases the conflicts between the generations: perhaps they can't agree about how important math is or about music or clothing styles or sexual behavior, and perhaps they verbally spar with one another left and right, but they can agree about sports and the necessity of being at the top of our game on Friday night, and they can come to recognize each other's humanity during the spirited faculty-student basketball game.

Similarly, sports can minimize conflict among students, who have to exist in close proximity despite having little in common in many cases, or perhaps even actively disliking one another. Sports can contribute to group cohesion when nothing else will. Maybe we can't stomach the guy, but he's *our* guy and can pound in twenty points a game.

Like all organizations, to keep themselves going schools have to build loyalty, transmit values that support their functioning, and maintain social control. The involuntary nature of schooling makes the loyalty and allegiance of students and controlling them major concerns of schools. Historically, academic programs have not proven to be particularly effective in bringing any of that about, so schools have looked to sports.

Interscholastic sports builds school spirit and loyalty through its promotion of an us-versus-them posture against opposing schools. Political leaders have long known that the way to elevate the allegiance of the populace is to get all of "us" on one side and all of "them" on the other. Being under siege and having to stand together or face the consequence of losing is a good stimulant to increased support from the subordinates.

More than that, athletics and athletes have an essentially conservative orientation. These activities, these people, are not typically the ones who will try to shake up the place or bring it to its knees. In sports, the school has an activity and a group of students who adhere to the values of the school: do what is set up for you to do and what those in authority tell you to do. Follow rules. Fit in. Work hard.

Also, sports can make teachers and administrators feel good. In sports, kids unquestioningly do what adults tell them to do. Instead of telling adults to get out of their lives, athletes willingly let adult referees swirl around them blowing whistles. In sports, kids dress the way they are told to, in uniforms, not in the faddish way they do the rest of the time.

It has been my experience that many men who go into education were serious sports participants when they were younger, and they are eager spectators now. Former school athletes can say to themselves, "Here are kids who are doing what I did at their age." Seeing someone doing what you did is comforting because it validates your experience. It would be tough to live with a situation in which students rejected or denigrated an activity you once participated in and still have a strong interest in. That would raise the question of whether you wasted your time in your youth and are still wasting it now watching pro football or whatever.

Another way that sports can make the adults feel good has to do with the anti-intellectual bias in schools. It is ironic that many who teach in our schools, places that are supposed to be about ideas, are uncomfortable around ideas, even a bit hostile to them. It is well documented that many teachers and administrators were not first-rate students themselves when they were in school. Whether measured by SAT scores, vocabulary tests, reading tests, or Graduate Record Examination scores, students majoring in education score well below the rest of the college population.[2] It is regrettable that the teaching profession doesn't attract more of those with top-tier academic talent and inclinations, and a number of reasons could be cited to account for that, among them how well teachers are paid and how well they are treated, including by students. But the fact remains that the chances are good that more than a few teachers feel greater comfort with the non-academic purposes and programs than they do with the academic ones. The prominence of sports in schools provides a counterbalance to a strict focus on academics that would make many educators feel uncomfortable. Sports makes it easier for teachers and administrators who are not truly engaged by intellectual activities to say, "Hey, I'm OK." School sports gives support to the idea that academics isn't everything, and may well not even be the most important thing, in school or in life generally.

Teachers face a lot of resistance and failure in their dealings with their students, more than a few of whom try their best to trivialize the educational enterprise. Faced with that reality, teachers are attracted to the rationalization, "Look, we don't have to get all that worked up about this stuff." Sports—the toy department of life—can be used to support that stance. Here is how it works: Taking sports seriously involves linking seriousness with something—sports—that can be legitimately viewed as inconsequential. To the extent that this kind of seriousness becomes a pattern, a norm, in a setting, it makes it easier for people in that setting to justify dealing with other things taken seriously there as if they too were fundamentally inconsequential. In this way, sports seriousness can serve to undercut taking anything in the school all that seriously, including academics.

As well as supporting a lack of seriousness about academics, sports legitimizes vicariousness. With sports, someone can be respected while doing nothing but watch others play the game. There is a great deal of vicariousness in teaching, talking about what other people are doing or have done—political leaders, generals, writers, and so forth. Teachers can start to feel a little funny about that: "What am *I* doing?" Sports holds that being an observer is altogether fine as long as you keep up on the central actors' exploits, care about how they do, and show up at the games. You don't have to play the game yourself to be okay.

Also, sports programs are consistent with the strong egalitarian strain that is prevalent in today's schools. Schools want everyone to be a success at something, and they are very relativistic about it. The success can be in just about anything that isn't directly anti-social. Sinking jump shots is just fine; so is crushing opposing linemen. Schools like to view everyone as an equal. They don't like elitism: "Don't forget, we are all equal here. You may be good at math, but Billy is a good linebacker, so it all evens out."

Schools emphasize good relationships and the group. They don't like people who aren't congenial and cooperative, and they don't like individualists. With its focus on the team as a unit and working together, sports provides for schools a positive example of how to conduct oneself in the classroom and elsewhere, and represents a very good argument against going off and doing business on your own.

There is strong pressure toward humility in schools—a value stressed in sports of course: "I couldn't have done it without my offensive line. And if it weren't for Coach Jones. . . ." Schools, public schools especially, want a student to get big, but not *too* big. Supporting sports does the job of helping keep the math whiz from getting too cocky. (How many quarterback sacks does *he* have?) At the same time, it helps the good athlete gain self-esteem, admiration from other youths, and inclusion in the group.

Sports adds drama and excitement to the lives of both students and faculty. I wouldn't exactly characterize school as a big adventure for most people who spend their time there—children or adults. In fact, school can be a downright dreary and contentious place at times. Anything that picks things up a bit is more than welcome.

Another reason for sports in schools is that the sports programs often serve as a unifying force for the community and increase the level of personal satisfaction for some of its members. Games are a place for adults to congregate and be with their neighbors. They provide excitement and entertainment, and are an occasion for nostalgic reminiscing. The success of school teams can be a source of identity, pride, and importance for people who have little of it elsewhere in their lives.[3]

As well, schools are a big part of the tax burden in most communities, and they are one of the few tax-supported services that all taxpayers can't share in equally. It makes good marketing sense for schools to provide something childless taxpayers can identify with.

Along the same line, when explaining the prominence of sports in schools, it also helps to understand that schools operate as a service industry that is highly responsive to consumer demand. Giving people what they want helps keep the large department store chains profitable, and it also helps schools keep themselves going. Just about anything an organized and vocal group wants from schools it will get if there is any way that the schools can do it without getting in deep trouble. Ask for an honors program, inclusion for the special education students, sex education, this club, that club—you've got it. As it turns out, often the most organized and vocal parents and members of the community are the ones who lobby in favor of school sports programs. It is not in the nature of schools to stand up to any group if they can help it; that just makes good public relations and survival sense. So if you want shiny football helmets, they're yours.

Moreover, schools can use sports programs as a club to protect and maintain themselves. If a school budget is threatened, the school can threaten right back, namely to cut athletic programs. One wonders how long this tactic will remain effective, however. We may start to see a response from the community: "Go ahead, cut sports or make kids pay to play—we've got other things to do with our money than sponsor football teams."[4]

And last, we can't forget that for a number of people, school sports is a way to make a living: for coaches, athletic directors, referees, game officials, team doctors, equipment manufacturers, and so on. Apart from its inherent worth, you can expect a strong argument for any activity that helps pay off the credit card.

CONCLUSION

Children get pushed and pulled to get into sports from every direction. They get into it because it is fun and exciting, it provides an opportunity to work on developmental issues, the media are hyping it, parents are promoting it, psychologists and other experts and conventional wisdom say it's important to do, and it appears to have future payoffs in terms of college admissions and career advancement. Add to all that the pressure schools put on children to take organized sports seriously and get involved. Parents—and children—need to understand how all of this works, because it can have important consequences for what children do and become in their lives.

Growing up, I never thought about any of this. Ball was to be played, and I played ball. Participating in sports had significant consequences for me, but it was not as if I foresaw those consequences and consciously sought to create or avoid them. I did not choose a way forward in my life from a clear sense of what else I could have done and become. I want parents and children to consciously chart the course of their own lives, in sports and every other area, and not simply become what outer forces and inner urges dictate.

CHAPTER 6

Girls in Sports

As you will recall, Ken Heise told me that he would very much like to see his daughter, Julie, play basketball, something she had shown promise in when she was younger. When I heard Ken say that, I thought to myself how times have changed. Not very long ago, Ken would have been far more likely to hold out the hope that Julie would become a basketball *cheerleader* rather than a basketball *player*; or he would have talked about her getting into something like dance or field hockey, a girls' activity. But not now.

FORCES FOR CHANGE

Three forces have been particularly influential in profoundly changing attitudes about girls' involvement in sports and promoting the burgeoning numbers of girls participating in organized athletics today.

First, there is the ideology of feminism. The women's movement has fostered womens' participation in what heretofore have been the domains of men. The movement has argued for the breakdown of what it considers to be the artificial and limiting distinctions between men and women. Feminist writers and activists have had a large impact on the way women define themselves—and are seen by others—in many areas, including politics, business, the family, and the arts. Since sports are subject to the same influences as every other aspect of life, the place of women in sports has been significantly affected by feminism in recent decades.

Second, the fitness movement contributes to changes in the way women look on their involvement in sports and athletic activities in general. The fitness movement exhorts men and women alike to become physically active, to get off the sidelines and into the game. There has been a deluge of books and articles in recent years on how to get in shape and eat right. New health clubs have sprung up. Sportswear and equipment ads portray attractive, sweating-but-satisfied women engaged in strenuous exercise and athletics. Girls and women have heard the call, as have those who set up programs for them.

A third force influencing women's sports is economics. I have found that very often one can make sense of what is going on in any area of society if one looks at it from the perspective of economic forces at work. Economic factors to some degree—and often to a large degree—shape everything else in our lives.

The biggest economic reality for girls growing up these days is the likelihood that they will work outside the home for most, if not all, of their adult lives. Indeed, this may well be as they want it: one of the tenets of our time is that fulfillment for women is tied to paid work. Whether or not personal satisfaction for women is associated with a career and bringing home a paycheck, however, economic realities alone will compel the majority of women to enter the work world, even if they marry. For most couples to make the mortgage payments, take a decent vacation, get the money together for the kids' college expenses, handle the increased tax burden, and put food on the table, both are going to have to be contributing money to the household. And given today's divorce and illegitimacy rates, young women frequently cannot count on there being a man around to contribute financially. They had better be ready to support themselves and their children on their own.

It could be that because women are going to work like men, this prompts them to play sports like men. Historically (I am thinking as far back as the 1890s or 1920s, or as recently as the 1940s or 1950s) when opportunities were provided for girls to play games and sports, the organizers designed activities that would cultivate what were considered to be womanly traits such as poise, body control, good form, health, and personal dignity. To modern sentiments that might sound quaint and even sexist, but apart from those considerations it also might be economically passé. Playing sports with those aims in mind probably does not resonate with the lives of girls who expect in a few years to be competing to get hired, maneuvering to attain career advancement, and setting up businesses.

Perhaps in this day and age, the historical rationales used to justify boys' sports programs will make more sense for girls. To illustrate, sports programs for middle-class boys were traditionally used to counteract the influences of what was considered to be women-dominated home lives. Participation in sports was seen as a way to turn overfeminized boys into assertive, competitive, achievement-oriented young men who could make their ways in the world. I am reminded of Ken's description (and what I took to be his worry) about his son David being a "hugger" and "momma's boy." I wonder if Ken's desire for a sports experience for David doesn't in part arise from his feeling that David needs to be toughened up a bit.

In contrast to its middle-class purpose, sports was historically viewed as a vehicle for taming working-class boys. It was thought that organized sports would make them more self-disciplined and responsive to authority in the kinds of jobs that were set out for them to do.[1] In present economic times, these two rationales for sports for boys—that a sports experience will harden and activate them and make them amenable to work life—may have increased appeal for girls. And the particular sports that are perceived to contribute most to those ends may look more attractive for them.

BOYS' SPORTS VERSUS GIRLS' SPORTS

Researchers have investigated how boys and girls differ in the way they participate in sports. The overall picture is of girls participating more for friendship and fun, whereas boys concentrate more on individual achievement and status. According to studies, boys are more outcomes-oriented, more concerned about the results they achieve, whereas girls are more focused on the process of the game. Boys show a stronger commitment to skill mastery, score higher in competitiveness, and are more oriented toward winning, while girls are more centered on relationships within the team. One study qualified that somewhat, however: its data suggested that girls' noncompetitiveness is due to a lack of experience in competitive sports, and that girls' demonstrated high achievement orientation in noncompetitive areas will carry over to sports as they are increasingly given the opportunity and encouragement to participate in competitive sports.[2]

Traditionally, organized sports for boys and for girls have differed from one another.[3] Think about what the following long-standing distinctions mean for girls getting into sports. Do these differences still hold true at this time? What are the trends—for instance, are girls' sports becoming more like boys' sports, or the other way around?

Traditionally, boys' sports have tended to be:

• *Specialized and elite.* The expectation is that the athletes have given serious attention to the requirements of the sport, practiced long and hard to prepare themselves, and bring talent and finely-honed skills to the undertaking.

- *Exclusive.* Only the best get to play. You try out for the team. You win a spot as a starter. Those who don't prevail in this process watch from the sidelines or sit on the bench.
- *Serious and intense.* The game is no casual affair, but rather a sober and all-out attempt to perform to the maximum of one's capability. Don't let anyone catch you taking the competition lightly. Athletes are trained to compete with their "game-faces" on—basically expressionless, but with the seriousness and formidability and determination showing through. There is room for celebration after a big play or a victory, but keep it brief and get back to business. There is a job to be done.
- *Formal.* Contests are tightly managed, with adult referees and umpires ever-watchful to make sure rules are followed to the letter.
- *Victory-oriented.* The focus is more on coming out on top in the score than on the process of the game or the players' experience during the game.
- *Risky and adventurous.* Something big is at stake. The excitement's up. It is akin to a trek into the jungle. You get pumped up for it.
- *Aggressive and dominance-oriented.* Your opponent is an enemy to be vanquished.
- *Public and spectatorial.* Publicized events with the results a matter of record, perhaps reported in the newspaper. People are expected to watch the games. In both schools and professional sports, potential spectators may be criticized for a lack of school spirit or poor team or community loyalty if they don't attend. (I have always been intrigued by the way professional sports can make people feel they have an obligation to go to their games. I am trying to think of what other commercial product can make you feel guilty for not buying it.)

In contrast to boys' sports, girls' sports have tended to be:

- *Held in balance with the other aspects of life.* In girls' sports there has been much less acceptance of the principle that you should give over virtually your whole being to perfecting your skills in a particular sport.
- *Inclusive.* Girls' sports have mostly operated from the premise that everyone should get to participate.
- *Less centered on performance and winning.* Girls' sports are viewed more as an educational and developmental experience for participants.
- *Private, less spectatorial.* Girls' sports have characteristically been an entertaining activity for the participants, but not an entertainment activity for others to enjoy.

- *Natural and spontaneous and oriented toward fun.* Characteristically, girls' sports have been friendly and cooperative, with the opponent viewed as the co-creator of the activity rather than an enemy to subdue.
- *Safer and more medically sound.* Girls and women have tended to play within or up to their limits, rather than constantly trying to exceed them.

It struck me as I was writing down these characteristics that when I was growing up it never occurred to me that organized sports could have any other attributes than what I associated with boys' sports. I'm sure I would have had more fun and actually done better if I had incorporated more of the orientation associated with girls' sports. I see now that I was unquestioningly carrying over an approach I had seen modeled by elite professional and college male athletes, for whom sports was a deadly serious, all-consuming business performed for the scrutiny and judgment of spectators. No wonder I got nervous before the games and was so tense during them.

Now that I think about it, it never occurred to me to relax and have a good time playing organized sports. After all, my high school basketball game was not exactly the seventh game of the NBA finals. Now I realize that the way I came at it was only one of several possibilities. It was not inherent in the plan of the cosmos that I spend every spare moment working on my jump shot or that I pace the locker room half sick to my stomach before a game. Indeed, the examples provided by girls' sports could lead to healthy changes in boys' sports if coaches and the boys themselves would see the advantages of these new options and selectively adopt some of the characteristics of girls' sports.

It can work the other way as well: as girls' sports cease to exist in a separate realm from boys' sports, girls will be able to gain a clearer perspective on the sports they play. They will be able to adopt some of the orientations and approaches employed in boys' sports, and use the example of boys' sports to enrich their own experiences in athletics. For example, girls may see—in fact many girls demonstrate that they already *do* see—how rewarding it can be to play in ways that until recently have been viewed as the province of boys: to push yourself to maximize your capability in your chosen sport, to compete intensely, to perform in the public arena, to shoot for victory with all you've got, to assert yourself vigorously head-to-head against an opponent, and to regard athletics as an adventure and risk.

Sport sociologist Jay Coakley thinks the increased participation of women in sports can be a vehicle for changing gender relations for the better. He notes that it could lead to an orientation among women toward doing over being, and activity over passivity. It could develop autonomy and assertiveness in women to balance out their supportiveness and nurturance of others. It could help women feel less vulnerable and more in control of their physical safety and psychological well-being. Sports could enhance among women the interpersonal skills needed for effectiveness in the public arena of society (e.g., in the work world, politics, the community). It could dampen any tendency women may have to conform to expectations based on presumed dependency and lack of competence. Also, sports could contribute to women taking their own aspirations seriously. It could counteract the image of girls as spectators and cheerleaders whose prime responsibility in life is to cheer on and support the exploits of men. Women in sports could do something to offset the bimbo-in-a-bikini advertising image that sports has fostered. Sports could help women see their bodies as instruments of power rather than as objects for the desires and pleasures of men. Sports could show that women are capable of physical work in occupations such as fire fighting, law enforcement, construction, and the military. Last, sports participation could provide women an opportunity to develop and express their talents.[4]

Beyond all that, women's sports simply allows women to do something many of them are interested in and want to do. It gives them the opportunity that men have had all along to do something that is challenging, fun, exciting, and invigorating. It gives them the chance to develop physical fitness. It gives them the chance to have the good relationships that go along with sports. It allows them to participate in a shared, communal activity, the dance that is sport competition at its best.

FIVE GIRLS IN SPORTS

I interviewed five girls active in high school sports to see how what they said squared with what I have been reading and observing. See what you can make of what they had to say.

Wendy

First was Wendy, a highly successful field hockey player. When I asked about how she became interested in sports, Wendy said her older brother, who is very successful in sports, was a model for her. She said her motives for getting into sports were to become part of a team, to meet people, and to make friends. As did several of the girls I interviewed (none of whom knew one another), Wendy talked about "bonding" with the other girls on the team. I was taken by the girls' use of that term. I didn't expect bonding to be part of their vocabulary, but it came up several times.

Throughout our talk, Wendy's focus remained on the team rather than on herself as an individual athlete. She always referred to herself within the context of the team. Wendy competes hard and very much wants to come out victorious, but she does it as a part of team and not as an individual. As for her individual achievement, she wants to be at her best and to be a "main contributor," as she put it, in order to best help the team succeed. As she sees it, both the competition and the outcome of the game demonstrate how the team is doing, how far it has progressed, not how she is doing. If Wendy, who is a star player, is serving any ego needs through sports, they appear to take a distant second place to her desire to support the collective effort.

Wendy spoke of the team being "only as good as the worst player." What that meant to her, she said, was that the girls on the team weren't there just to play their games and cooperate with the other players; they have the job of encouraging and supporting the improvement of every other player, especially those who are less talented. As Wendy talked, I recalled back to my own experience in boys' sports, where by and large everybody was left to get it together on their own. We certainly didn't go around propping up the worst players on the team; at best, we silently endured them.

As much as Wendy wants the team to be successful, it became clear that at least as high a priority for her is the experience she and her fellow players have during the game. Wendy said that a major reason that she wants to do well is so that others will have a good experience and come to love field hockey as much as she does. She talked of times when "everything is clicking" for the team, which means that everyone is working together and it is "flowing," as she put it. She also talked about loving the times when the intensity of the game takes over and everything else, including issues and concerns in other parts of her life, fades into the background.

I had no sense from talking to Wendy that she views sports as a way to achieve social status in the school, become popular, meet boys, any of that. Rather, she is oriented toward the quality of the relationships she establishes with others on her team. Wendy spoke glowingly about the friendships she has formed through sports. She said she feels more connected to others through sports. There is more intensity in these relationships and more honesty. You can't hide or fake it, she said. Wendy said she feels she can trust her teammates completely, share any confidence with them. She talked about how great it is to be with her teammates, how much fun she has with them, and how she can count on them for anything. She said that the relationships she has formed are so important to her that she doesn't want to play an individual sport such as tennis.

As I was talking with Wendy, I thought about the investigations Harvard University psychologist Carol Gilligan made into the relationships among adolescent girls.[5] Gilligan and her colleagues found that relationships among girls are often characterized by a large measure of inauthenticity. That is to say, girls are not quite real with one another. It is as if to be with other girls, to be included and accepted by them, you have to give up part of yourself. You have to censor or suppress who you really are. You have to give up your own voice, as it were. You can't know what you know, and say and do what is true for you. For many girls, being who you really are, all that you are, seems too big a risk to take. It can result in being disliked, condemned, or excluded by others. There isn't enough trust in their relationships with other girls to take the chance of revealing their true selves. The result is that the person others know and accept isn't the real person. The relationships Gilligan describes are not as personally satisfying as girls would like, nor do they properly support girls in defining and living out who they are as individuals.

The sorts of relationships Gilligan found were not what Wendy was describing with her teammates. Perhaps being part of a shared undertaking and in relationships that have a purpose outside of the relationships themselves create a context for truer and more satisfying connections for Wendy.

Although Wendy's sports involvement centers on her relationships with her teammates, other associations count for her as well. Her brother is now a hockey player at West Point, and Wendy radiated as she spoke of a time when she overheard him telling his friends how proud he is of her accomplishments in sports. She also talked of how her parents come to the games and how much that means to her, and how bad she feels about friends' parents not attending the games.

Wendy draws a distinction between men's and women's sports. She said she likes to watch men's hockey but personally doesn't like the idea of women playing sports such as hockey and football. Wendy places a value on fluid and beautiful movement for girls, but not roughness. It became clear that Wendy has a well-defined conception of what is natural and appropriate for men and women in sports. She isn't strident about it, but she knows where she stands and she conducts her life accordingly.

Caroline

My second interview was with Caroline, a student at a private school and a rower. Both Caroline's father and older brother are enthusiastic and accomplished rowers, and Caroline sees rowing as part of a family identity. As does Wendy, Caroline seeks out competition, but with the focus being on competition as part of a group. *We* are competing, not *I* am competing. Caroline sees competition as a way to prove hers is the best rowing team, whether it is in doubles, fours, or eights. Even though Caroline very much wants to win, she focuses even more on the experiences she has while rowing. She said she loves the feeling of physical exhaustion, and she spoke of being addicted to the flow of the contest, to "flying," as she put it.

Caroline also values the close relationships she forms with her teammates. She described these relationships as intense, and I thought again about how that contrasts with the constrained relationships Gilligan found in her research. Caroline said she had not joined the rowing team as a way of becoming a star in the school. Unlike Wendy, Caroline isn't drawn to what she considers to be "girl sports" such as lacrosse and soccer. She said these sports are too "wimpy" and have "a lot of little special rules of what you can and can't do." She wants rigor and discipline and to be treated the same way as the boys. She spoke of the rowing team at another school where there aren't high expectations and good discipline and where the girls are "bitchy—like small yappy dogs" and "more interested in what they look like than anything else." No matter how much she loves rowing, she wouldn't stay on a team like that, Caroline said.

Jackie

Jackie, a lacrosse player, told me that an early influence spurring her interest in sports came when she discovered her athletic ability in gym class. She was consistently chosen to captain teams and she could run faster than the boys.

Jackie sees herself as an athlete but not a jock. Those are different identities to her. Jackie is strongly committed to her own athletic excellence, but she seeks to be the most effective player possible so that she can best contribute to the team's success. Jackie definitely wants to win—she is not in the sport merely to participate—yet her focus is not on her own personal victories but rather on those of the team. She said she didn't want to mess up because it would harm the team.

Jackie particularly values the experience of running with fluidity and grace as a lacrosse player. She draws a distinction between masculine and feminine sports, saying that she is on a "girly" lacrosse team. Jackie spoke of the difference between the style of the team she is on and that of another school. She said the other team did not maintain their femininity. Jackie sees a qualitative difference between flowing, beautiful movement and a scrambling, rough approach to the game.

She said it was alright with her if other girl athletes were that way, but it wasn't for her and her teammates.

Jackie spoke warmly of the relationships she has formed in lacrosse: "I love it because I love the people I play with." She too referred to bonding with her teammates. Even though running speed is her prime asset, Jackie said she won't go out for track because she doesn't see the bonding there. She said she doesn't have relationships like the ones with her lacrosse teammates anywhere else in her life. She talked about the closeness she feels, how straightforward the relationships are, how she isn't embarrassed, and how she can tell it like it is and ask for advice. She loves how everyone is focused on a common goal and loves being immersed in the endeavor. "It doesn't matter who you are," she said—which I took to mean that everyone matters because they are all part of the collective effort. In sports, you aren't alone: "If you fall, there are ten other people to pick you up," Jackie said.

Although the relationships with her teammates are her major concern, Jackie does feel she gets more attention for being in lacrosse. She cited being more popular and getting invited to more parties as examples of that.

Jackie has some difficulties in school, and she said that one good thing about sports is that you can get caught up in the game and forget your other troubles, "like in math."

Jackie has high praise for her parents. She describes her father as having "unbending principles." To him, there are things that need to be done no matter what. But although her father lets Jackie know he wants her to achieve, at the same time she doesn't feel pressured by him. Jackie described her parents as "having me do everything to see how I liked it," listing ice skating, gymnastics, and ballet as examples. Jackie said her parents gave her the chance to achieve, not just participate. They gave her opportunities in sports and went with what she was good at. Jackie said that is the tack she will take with her own children someday: provide them with as many opportunities as possible and then push it in the areas where they excel.

Gretchen

Gretchen is on the field hockey team and is a star softball pitcher. She said she doesn't like field hockey as much because at her school it is "all serious and not social enough." Gretchen said she has grown up in a town that "lives for sports," and that an older brother was formally a star football player and is now on the Yale team. She said the main reason she got into sports was because her friends were involved. Gretchen describes herself as a social person and smiled as she recounted the time they decorated the bus that took everyone to a softball game, the big pasta dinners they have, and how the boys and girls go to each others' games.

Gretchen said she likes sports, but she won't live for them. She described them as fun, plus she is good at them, and that is mainly why she is involved. She likes to compete, which to her means competing as a part of a team and winning. She likes being on a team where everyone shares the same goals. She spoke of her coach saying "A team is only as good as its weakest player," which to her means that you can't just rely on one or two stars; everyone on the team matters. Gretchen's orientation is toward helping the team win and not individual achievement, even though several times her softball pitching has been featured in newspaper accounts of her games. She emphasized the importance of contributing to team unity and working on her skills to be able to best help the team win. To Gretchen, there definitely is an *I* in team; but it is an *I* contributing to a *we*. When I asked about her softball pitching, Gretchen said she isn't doing it for ego or personal satisfaction. When she does well, she said, it makes everyone on the team happy, and her parents too.

When I asked what it was like to compete, Gretchen very quickly answered, "You have to block out everything and be aware of everything." I took that to mean that you have to be in the moment, sensitive to everything that is happening right now, and at the same time leave the rest of your life out of it.

Gretchen said that girls want to have fun in sports and make it an event, whereas boys are more critical of one another and don't want a kid who isn't very good to play. Boys seem to be more oriented toward individual success, she speculated. Although girls care about how they do, she said, they are most focused on team success.

Gretchen said if she has a daughter some day, she will try to get her involved in all sorts of activities, including sports. The object of that will be to find out what her daughter likes and what she is good at. If her daughter chooses to pursue sports, Gretchen said, she will tell her to be a team player because personal satisfaction is greater if the team wins. She will warn her daughter about becoming big-headed about her successes. Gretchen spoke of a star on her team whom nobody likes because she isn't modest. Gretchen said if her child isn't very good at sports, she will say, "If it makes you happy, stay on the team," but at the same time Gretchen will try to introduce new possibilities to her.

Heather

Heather was the last person I spoke to. She is one of the best track sprinters in the state and also plays field hockey. She said she has two older brothers who have played football and basketball.

When Heather was in elementary school, a friend of the family was the coach of the seventh grade field hockey team and invited Heather to play. Heather asked another girl to check out the possibility with her.

Heather's orientation toward sports contrasts with that of the other girls I spoke with. Her focus isn't so much on the social relationships she forms through sports. Rather, it is on having fun and competing. For Heather, competition doesn't mean competing to win as part of a team. Instead, it means competing against herself to improve on her previous performance. Heather is trying to improve her times in track. She said that she chose to wear her track jacket because she is better in track than she is in field hockey. She said she doesn't play basketball because she isn't good at it. Heather said that she thinks her approach to sports is more like that of a boy, and that maybe that is because of all of the time she spent playing sports with her brothers as she was growing up.

Heather said that when she is a parent she thinks she will push sports more with her daughter than her parents have done with her. "Even if your daughter isn't very good at sports?" I asked. "If she enjoyed it, yes, I would still push it," Heather replied.

Reviewing what these girls reported, four of the five seemed to be quite similar in their orientation, with Heather differing somewhat from the others. These girls care about skill development and individual achievement, but not as a way to attain stardom, status, or notoriety. Development and achievement are either a means to the end of contributing to the team or, in Heather's case, in support of her goal of surpassing her current level of performance. There is the strong focus on relationships. This didn't show up in the interview with Heather, however, except in her account of asking a friend to go with her to the first field hockey practice. All five girls are competitive, although not as an individual against other individuals. The first four are competitive as part of a larger whole, the team, and on behalf of the team, and Heather is competitive against herself. Except for Heather, the girls I spoke to emphasize the experience of playing—the intensity and flow of the game and competing alongside their teammates. But they also care about outcomes. Certainly the first four care about winning, although, again, not as individuals; it is the team that they want to win. Although she didn't say so explicitly, my guess is that Heather is also committed to winning over others, whether as an individual or as part of a team. But she also considers herself to have won—or at least experienced satisfaction—if she exceeds her own previous standard even if she doesn't outrace an opponent or her team doesn't come out victorious. You can see the influences of family—parents and brothers—in all these girls. Each distinguished between masculinity and femininity in sports, although the particular meaning differs from one to another. And they all participate in sports from a clear sense of how their involvement relates to their gender.

To put these interviews in perspective, let me report the comments of three boys I spoke to recently. Jeff and Nathan are basketball players, and Tom plays football. Much of what they said echoed what the girls reported, especially when they talked about contributing to the team and how much they value the relationships they have formed through sports. But there were differences as well. Jeff said that even if his team wins, if he doesn't play well he is disappointed. He told me he is thinking of quitting the high school basketball team because the coach is starting to rotate him with another player. Nathan said that if he scored twenty points and the team lost he'd be basically happy, although he would still be down a bit because he would want the team to win and everyone to feel good. And if it were the other way around, Nathan said, and he scored only three points and the team won, he'd be glad the team won, but, although he would try not to show it, he would be mostly upset because he is there to achieve as an individual. Tom told me that a big part of his motivation to play high school football is that it makes him part of an elite group in school, that he is looked up to and respected more now that he's on the team. Tom also said that sports is taking priority over academics and his schoolwork is suffering. None of this was the sort of thing I heard from any of the girls.

I am impressed by the way the five girls I talked to participate in sports. I see much that is healthy about what they are doing. Sports seems to be contributing to their development as people and not detracting from it. They keep sports in perspective, in balance with their other involvements; sports is just one of a number of things they do. I like how they care about both the process and the outcome of their games. They appreciate the beauty and flow of the contest, the quality of the ongoing experience of playing sports. They see participation in the activity as an end in itself and not just as a means to an end. At the same time, they care about skill development and competition and achievement and winning.

These girls do not lose sight of the fact that they are young women, not young men. They don't presume they have to think and act like men to participate in sports. I am reminded of a comment by 1994 Olympic figure skating gold medalist, Oksana Baiul. She said that her model is American skater Jill Trenary, who Oksana said maintained her femininity while competing and expressed her womanhood through her skating. Oksana said she seeks to move with grace and beauty and to compete and win as a woman. I heard that same sentiment being expressed by several of the girls I spoke with—which is not to say that Baiul's is the only legitimate perspective in skating or any other sport, and several of my interviewees pointed that out. It is, however, an affirmation of the differences between men and women, and of women playing sports in ways that are natural and uplifting to them.

In their book, *Sociology of North American Sport*, sport sociologists D. Stanley Eitzen and George Sage cite the outcomes of a study of 669 female athletes that found that participation in sports was modestly related to popularity, slightly related to educational aspiration, and not related to psychological well-being, self-esteem, sociability, academic achievement, or sex-role attitudes.[6] My guess is that the research findings reported by Eitzen and Sage generally fit the girls I interviewed; but I would also guess that they would be beside the point to them. That is, I am not sure these girls care whether sports contributes to their popularity or educational aspirations just as long as it doesn't detract significantly from them (and I had no indication that sports did that in their cases). These girls really aren't involved in sports to be popular. They are in sports to experience relationships that are better than they could get anywhere else. Perhaps boys connect sports with popularity and social status, but as far as I could tell the girls I spoke to don't. As for psychological well-being, the girls seem to me to be very balanced human beings and don't appear to be looking for sports to boost their psychological health or self-esteem. And these girls seem comfortable with their sociability, including the quieter, more removed Heather, who appears to accept her lack of gregariousness. As for sex-role attitudes, the girls bring relatively articulate and, as far as I am concerned, defensible and personally constructive sex-role perspectives with them to sports, and they participate in sports in a way that is consistent with these attitudes. And last, although I didn't press them on it, my sense is that consistent with the finding reported by Eitzen and Sage, sports has little effect on the level of academic accomplishments of these girls.

THE FUTURE OF GIRLS' SPORTS

As for the future of girls' sports, the trend in the society has been toward blurring gender distinctions, and because sports is intricately linked to the rest of life, it will likely reflect this trend. For several decades women have been growing more assertive, and this could manifest itself in the ways girls participate in sports. The result may be that girls' sports take on more of the characteristics of boys' sports. The adoption of some of the characteristics associated with boys' sports may well have a positive influence on girls' sports. It may broaden the options available to women in the kinds of sports they play and in the manner in which they play. On the other hand, girls might get caught up in the specialization and elitism that characterize boys' sports and restrict opportunities to participate. Some of the fun might disappear from girls' sports. A focus on results might deflect girls from the joy that accompanies the flow of the game. Girls might increasingly see themselves as having to be number one even if it detracts from other areas in their life, including academics. Girls might start to think that their only option is personal sacrifice and total dedication to sports, and that might lead them to deny their emotions and connections to other people and to think that success on the field is worth any price, including taking drugs to enhance performance, playing in pain, being aggressive and playing dirty, and seeing the competition as an enemy to dominate and vanquish instead of as a partner in the experience.

One factor that has affected the way girls approached sports in the past has been the lack of opportunities for women to continue in their sport after they leave school. There have been professional women's golf and tennis, a few ice-skaters have made it big financially with endorsements and ice shows, and women have played professional basketball in Europe. But women's athletics has not been nearly as professionalized and commercialized as men's sports have. The result has been that few girls have viewed themselves as future professional athletes in training. However, that could be changing. In 1996 the American Basketball League got off the ground in this country, and in 1997 the NBA embarked on an effort to make woman's professional basketball a success here. The National Soccer Alliance would like to make a go of a women's first-division professional league. These highly publicized efforts and others like them will bring visibility to women professional athletes and, perhaps, what has gone along with it in men's sports. From earliest childhood, boys are deluged by images of glamorous professional athletes. Professional sports knows what the movie industry knows: stars sell tickets (as well as shoes, jackets, soft drinks, and breakfast cereal) and put people in front of television sets. In our economy, getting paid a great deal of money contributes to one's public image as a star. Professional sports teams make certain that everyone knows what their players are paid. The fact that someone makes 10 million dollars a year to play baseball gives weight to the activity. A byproduct of all the commercial activity surrounding professional sports is that large numbers of 8- and 12- and 16-year-old boys are left starry-eyed and thinking, "Hey, playing pro sports is *the* thing to do—and look at all the money that goes along with it."

Will girls get hooked into the "I'm going to be a sports star and make the big money" fantasy in the same way so many boys do? As elite women athletes catch the public eye, increasingly girls might think, "That could be me!" Indeed, the example of top women athletes might expand the possibilities for women to enrich their experience (and their bank accounts) and achieve in sports far beyond the limitations within which they have heretofore operated. But then again, the increased commercial success of women professional athletes could lead girls to premature exposure to the rigors of the adult world and to the excesses we see in men's sports. We will have to keep an eye on it to see which way it goes.

In the spring of 1997, the President's Council on Physical Fitness and Sports issued a highly publicized report, *Physical Activity and Sport in the Lives of Girls*, which maintains that exercise and sport improves virtually every aspect of girls' lives, including their schoolwork, social adjustment, and mental and physical health. The report recommends that girls be encouraged from an early age to get involved in sports and physical activity, and that there be required daily physical education in schools and increased funding for after-school and community-based programs of exercise, health, and athletics.

Despite the solid reputations of the authors of the various sections of the report and the strong endorsement the report received from the Secretary of Health and Human Services and others, there is some question of how seriously to take its findings and recommendations. For one thing, one wonders about bias. The stated purpose of the President's Council is to be a "catalyst to promote, encourage, and motivate the development of physical activity, fitness, and sport participation for all Americans."[7] Plus, sports and physical education professionals are prominently represented on the Council and among the authors of the report. That doesn't mean that the report is slanted necessarily, but it does send up the signal to review what it says carefully.

A major problem with the report stems from its reliance on correlational research evidence. For example, the report's summary states: "Sports are an educational asset for girls' lives. Research findings show that many high-school athletes report higher grades and standardized test scores, and lower dropout rates, and are more likely to go on to college than their non-athletic counterparts."[8] I suspect the authors of the report would not be overly disappointed if the reader inferred that sports involvement caused this difference among girls (the section of the report that cites the actual research never establishes that) and that the difference is a big one (it isn't). As was pointed out in Chapter 3, youngsters who go out for sports teams might simply be better students to begin with, and a difference that is statistically significant (big enough for a researcher to justify the conclusion that it is a real one and not due to a random or chance fluctuation) may be so small that it has little or no practical importance.

Another problem, the report consistently refers to good things that *can* happen as a result of physical activity and sports. Of course that is not the same as saying that they *will* happen, and thus the question remains as to how often they actually *do* happen. The vast majority of the time? Fifty percent of the time? Twenty percent? Or is it like the lottery that one *can* win, but likely not in this lifetime. And is physical activity/sports—one or the other or both, whichever it is, the report isn't always clear on this point—the only way these positive outcomes can occur? In the mental health area, for instance, does it have to be exercise and/or sports, or might talk therapy or joining a youth group at church accomplish the same purpose? And last, what about the *bad* things that the report acknowledges can occur as a consequence of girls' involvement in sports, among them, eating disorders, stress and anxiety, and increased tolerance for aggression?

After reading the report, I am left with the common sense conclusion that a reasonable amount of physical activity in one's life is a good idea, and that that could take the form of informal activities such as swimming with the family, rowing a boat, rollerblading, playing soccer with friends, or jogging. Beyond that, more organized involvements, I think it is a matter of a lifestyle choice, one that is sometimes rewarding in varying degrees and sometimes unrewarding in varying degrees. I certainly don't share the President's Council's eagerness to tax people to pay for more physical education and sports programs. As far as I am concerned, if people want to go that route, fine, but I don't see it as urgent business.

When you think about your daughter and who she is and where she is going, and about particular sports for her, you'll find there are many possibilities. Thinking back to what Jackie said, perhaps the only way you and your daughter will ever really know which sports are most appropriate is for your daughter to try the ones that seem most promising and see what results. There are competitive sports such as softball, tennis, volleyball, basketball, soccer, swimming, field hockey, gymnastics, and fencing. There are martial arts such as tai chi, aikido, and karate that develop confidence, balance, and physical presence. Ballet and jazz and modern dance contribute to body alignment, grace and dignity of movement, and physical expressiveness. There are noncompetitive sports—although some of them are competitive at times—such as archery, bowling, jogging, skating, golf, tennis, and riding. And there are outdoor activities such as camping, hiking, climbing, hunting, and fishing. Both you and your daughter and Ken and his daughter, Julie, have some good alternatives to contemplate.

CHAPTER 7

Social Class, Race, and Sports

Caroline, one of the girls I interviewed for Chapter 6, is from an upper-class background, and both she and her brother became rowers. Heather, one of the other interviewees, is from a working-class background and became a track sprinter. The fact that Caroline took up rowing and Heather got into track may be more than a matter of chance or personal preference. As I talked to the two girls, it seemed clear that their socioeconomic status has played a significant part in determining the form of athletic involvement each has chosen, including the fact that Caroline's private school, which caters to wealthier students, has a crew team and Heather's public school does not. Speaking with them prompted me to reflect on my own situation. How much of my father's hopes for me to become a professional baseball player was a function of our lower-class background? If I had grown up in a different socioeconomic circumstance, would my experience and outlook and relationship to sports have been different? I think the answer is yes, and I am left to speculate on how that would have made my life different, and not just in sports.

We don't talk about social class very much in relation to sports. For that matter, because the notion of class distinctions runs against our egalitarian ideals, most of us are uncomfortable thinking or talking about class in any context. We avoid the topic; what we don't attend to doesn't exist for us. Nevertheless, one can't fully understand sports without taking social class differences into account.

Although participation in the various sports frequently crosses class lines, it is not accurate to say that all Americans play the same games.[1] Consider the following clusters of sports and take note of what images come to mind: yachting and equestrian; golf and tennis;

football, basketball, baseball, and hockey; bowling and auto racing. Think about pool versus squash. The meanings these sports have can rub off on those who take part in them. Involvement in a sport can reinforce social class identities, which are reference points for life-styles, aspirations, and expectations. And that includes spectators: What does it mean for someone to attend motorcycle races, or to sit in exclusive sky boxes at a baseball or football game rather than the cheap seats?

Indeed, class does matter when talking about sports. So does race. For that matter, so do ethnicity and religion and geography, but due to space restriction (this is an enormous topic, a book in itself) I will limit this discussion to class and race, and within race only refer to African Americans, a group very prominent in many sports. I hope the discussion of the relationship of social position and race to sports in the next pages encourages the Heises and you to think more deeply about the significance of these factors in relation to their own situation.

Looking at sports from the perspective of class and race opens new concerns. An example: I have become intrigued with what is going on in basketball. Over the years, basketball has increasingly become associated with low-income, inner-city African-American youth. Perhaps it is coincidental, but organized basketball, especially at the high school and college levels, is more and more looking to me like the referees' show, as they swarm about and descend on the action every few seconds to chastise and control the players. It is as if the players are irresponsible children who must be forced to behave, or lesser individuals who must be controlled.

I am trying to think of another sport where the rules are violated forty or fifty times a game. I watch kids in the playground playing spirited basketball and there is a foul or other rules violation every once in a while, but they seem to be getting on with the game. It has gotten to the point where fouling has become a central part of organized basketball. Strategic fouling at the end of games slows things to a crawl and turns it into a free-throw shooting contest. Teams run plays at each other's stars with the intent of getting them out of the game, knowing that it's tough not to get called for a foul unless you stand stock-still, feet planted, arms at your side, and fall over like a freshly cut redwood tree when touched; "taking a charge" it's called. How often does a player in foul trouble step aside and not even contest a jump shot or layup because he knows that more likely than not he will pick up a foul no matter what he does? If he complains, if he doesn't defer immediately to the authority of the referee—most often a middle-aged white man (am I overreacting?)—that's a technical foul. Basketball is a beautiful game, but to me it is becoming characterized by the action stopping dead and the players dutifully standing quietly aside while a player shoots a free throw at the direction of the referee. I ask myself, is this intense scrutiny, management, and domination of the players inherent in the game of basketball, or does it have something to do with who is playing the game?

It is important to think about how parents socialize their children into sports they consider to be the most appropriate given the family's social position. The question to ask yourself is how much your own social conditioning and socioeconomic status influence your children's sports involvement and your hopes for them relative to sports. Researcher Gai Berlage studied the parents of 11- and 12-year-old ice hockey players. Berlage found that 57 percent of the fathers from the lower socioeconomic class hoped their sons would play professional hockey, while only 5 percent of the fathers from the highest socioeconomic class expressed this aspiration.[2]

There is also the impact of the example parents set for their children. Ken Heise asked whether parents being active in sports goes along with their children getting involved. There does seem to be evidence of this. One study found that a high percentage of the fathers and mothers of young female athletes were actively engaged in athletics themselves,[3] and I would assume that this holds true for male athletes as well. Assuming that the parents' sports participation reflects their social class position and that this is the model of sports involvement their children are exposed to, it is another way children's engagement in sports is shaped by their social class backgrounds.

As for African Americans, there is evidence that a very high percentage of black athletes aspire to professional sports careers as compared to other groups. One study showed that 43 percent of black high school athletes expect to play sports professionally—a remarkably high percentage.[4] It is very likely that cultural factors play a part in these expectations. John Hoberman in his book *Darwin's Athletes* notes that an emphasis on athletic accomplishment permeates the black community to the point that other endeavors are devalued. Hoberman points out that well-known African-American sociologist Harry Edwards has gone so far as to declare that the highest form of human genius is athleticism.[5] Hoberman argues that the stress on sports among blacks has been in large measure conditioned by white racist disparagement of black intelligence and stereotypes of black physicality. It is likely that the interest in sports careers among American blacks is also influenced by their perception that other avenues for self-expression and financial reward are closed off to them. Social class is undoubtedly a factor as well. Many blacks have low-income backgrounds and share with low-income whites the outlook characteristic of their common socioeconomic class. I haven't been able to find research on how the sports involvements and aspirations of lower-class blacks compare to those of upper-class blacks. I suspect that lower-class blacks have higher hopes for a sports career than upper-class blacks do.

Many elements that constitute the outlook of people from lower socioeconomic groups have an impact on their orientation toward sports, but I want to talk about one phenomenon that I see as particularly important. I call it the *Major Bowes* world view. This is an esoteric reference, but I will explain.

Major Bowes was the host of a radio show in the 1930s called *The Original Amateur Hour*, something like the *Star Search* television show of recent years. On the *Amateur Hour*, entertainment acts would compete to win the chance to come back for another week and attain stardom in show business. This was during the depth of the Depression, and the *Amateur Hour* became a metaphor that represented people hitting it lucky and getting out of the hole they were in. Perhaps today the lottery carries this same hope—the masses' only chance to escape the fix they are in. Buy a lottery ticket and get a buck's worth of hope. That is what the Major Bowes show came to symbolize in those tough times—hope for people who had little or none of it otherwise. Those listening to the Amateur Hour were able to vicariously experience people transcending their predicaments in a dramatic way.

Hitting it big by becoming a sports star has been a recurring theme over the years. Many sports heroes come from humble backgrounds. I remember as a kid reading time and again about big-time sports stars saying, "If it hadn't been for sports I'd be working in the mines"—or pumping gas or in prison, something to that effect. I got the idea that if they *had* eventually wound up pumping gas it would have been acceptable to them because they had had their shot at the big time. The assumption behind their comments seemed to be that if you come from a modest background all you can ask for is one chance at stardom. If you don't make it, it is a lunch pail job for you, and that is the way it is supposed to be.

The statements by these sports stars reflected what I call a Major Bowes worldview. That is, for them there was no middle ground, such as starting a business, learning a skilled trade, or becoming a doctor or lawyer. It was either stardom and riches through sports or staying at the bottom of the social heap—nothing in between. Within my own lower social class circumstances, it seemed that for someone like me, as far out of the core of American life as I was, as unentitled as I was, it was sports or nothing much at all, and I believe that served to accelerate my personal investment in playing sports at that time.

A Major Bowes perspective in a child, or in parents, may produce a millionaire star athlete, but it may also distract a child from what he or she needs to develop fully as a unique individual. It may seriously diminish the child's chances for a good life as an adult. Fantasizing a professional or college sports career is an unrealistic ambition for the vast majority of youngsters, and it can get in the way of preparing themselves for a more attainable future. Sport sociologist Richard Lapchick computed the odds of a high school athlete making it to the pros in football, baseball, and basketball by comparing the number of high school athletes with the number entering the pros in a given year.[6] For football, the odds of making it to the pros are 6,318 to 1; for basketball 10,345 to 1; and for baseball 7,325 to 1—all very long odds indeed. What would send the odds even higher would be to compute the odds against having a *successful* sports career. Lapchick only takes into account those who get signed by the pros. Most athletes who play pro ball have "a cup of coffee," as they say. They last a year or two, if that. As for the chances of playing college athletics, the fact is that there are about forty-three times as many high school football players as Division I college players.[7]

The assumption among many people is that professional sports is the way out of the ghetto for black youth. With, as Lapchick reports, the odds of a black athlete making the pros in basketball being 7,622 to 1,[8] one can't help but conclude that a professional sports career is a realistic goal for precious few African Americans. And if 43 percent of young black athletes think they are going to make it through sports, this represents a very serious problem.

History tells us there is a way to make it in America, and it is not through dreams of stardom. It is through the development of personal responsibility, self-discipline, and industriousness, and through support from family and church and others in your group, and through exploiting to the maximum whatever educational opportunities are available—and, of course, an athletic scholarship is just that. Sports needs to be viewed as one among many possible contributions to that process.

We allow, even encourage, minority and poor kids to chase after dreams that will end up shattered. As a society, we should look at the effects of holding up the lucky few in sports and entertainment as examples for our children. Anything you can do as a parent to bring a sense of personal responsibility and a realistic outlook into your child's life will help, and that includes realistic career ambitions. What makes parenting such a challenge and such an art is that while you are being realistic, you also have to avoid being the parent who tells a young Damon Stoudamire (a five-foot-ten-inch star in the NBA) that people his size are too small for the NBA and that he ought to think about being an accountant.

Many contend that athletics improves minority youngsters' school grades, keeps them in school, and raises their educational expectations. They see sports as helping minority youngsters learn to aspire higher, work harder, sacrifice, and overcome obstacles in pursuit of academic success. Detractors, on the other hand, assert that sports deflects minority students' time and energy from the classroom.

Researchers Merrill Melnick, Donald Sabo, and Beth Vanfossen explored the merits of these arguments as they investigated the educational effects of interscholastic athletic participation on 3,686 African American and Hispanic youths.[9] The Melnick, Sabo, and Vanfossen study showed that sports participation is a social resource for minority students. Minority athletes see themselves as more popular and socially active, and they participate more in extracurricular activities than their non-athletic peers. However, this brings up the chicken-and-egg question: Did these students become more popular and active because of sports, or did the fact they were popular and active in the first place push them into sports?

Even though sports may give minority students a social boost according to the Melnick, Sabo, and Vanfossen study, it doesn't appear to help academically. Their data showed that sports involvement had little effect on grade-point average and educational expectations. In these areas, athletes were similar to non-athletes. Of course that doesn't rule out the possibility that sports might have kept athletes from doing worse in school than they would otherwise have done. I suspect this is the case in some instances, but fewer than is commonly believed. On the plus side, Melnick, Sabo, and Vanfossen found the academic record of minority athletes was at least equal to that of comparable non-athletes, which they say contradicts the "dumb jock" stereotype.

Interestingly enough, Melnick, Sabo, and Vanfossen found that high school sports doesn't prevent dropouts. It must be remembered, however, that this conclusion is a statistical generalization. Sports undoubtedly does keep some minority students in school. Nevertheless, the Melnick, Sabo, and Vanfossen findings raise doubts about the popular contention that if it weren't for sports, many more youngsters would drop out. People may be overgeneralizing from the few clear instances where sports is in fact holding a young person in school. And, of course, the fact that youngsters stay in school and graduate doesn't necessarily mean they took advantage of the opportunity to learn something while they were there. The sad truth is that a high school diploma is often in reality only a certificate of attendance.

Melnick, Sabo, and Vanfossen point out that with all the forces bearing in on minority youth in the city—including crime, poverty, and drug abuse—it is unrealistic to expect sports alone to turn them around. They say that to assign sports more significance than their findings reveal is to run the risk of oversimplifying and trivializing the very complex psychological and sociological processes that accompany minority high school athletic participation. Melnick, Sabo, and Vanfossen conclude that the impact of sports has been overestimated in both directions: sports is neither a powerful resource for minority students nor the treadmill to oblivion that some critics allege.

The widely held perception that athletics paves the way to college for African-American youngsters needs to be examined critically. It is important to remember that what is most important is not going to college; it is *succeeding* there. If college success is the criterion, then it is important to ask whether black—or any other, for that matter—high school athletes are developing the academic wherewithal to get a college degree. What if they get to college and aren't the star of the team? What if the friendship and popularity that came through sports in high school doesn't continue? Will they quit school? Have they developed the inner resources to persist in their college studies when those social and athletic props are absent? Have these young people learned to find meaning and satisfaction in intellectual activities and developed enough academic drive to plug on when the going gets tough in their courses? Has sports distracted them from becoming true students of the sort I described in Chapter 3—self-reliant questers after increased knowledge and intellectual capability? As you can tell, I have my doubts.

Researchers Eldon Snyder and Elmer Spreitzer investigated how participation in sports among minority students affects college attendance.[10] The single major positive effect of sports on college attendance that Snyder and Spreitzer found was among students who have what they call a "lower degree of cognitive development"; that is to say, among the students with the least academic talent. The Snyder and Spreitzer study suggests that sports has the biggest impact on college attendance among the students who are the least capable and who presumably would have been the least disposed to pursue further academic education.

The fact that athletics encourages students to go to college who would not otherwise have done so could be viewed as a good thing; but then again, it reminds us that athletic scholarships often put resources into the students who are the least likely to make the best of the assistance. In data compiled in 1997 by the National Collegiate Athletic Association, the graduation rate for black male college basketball players was 39 percent compared to the rate of the 56 percent of the general student body. The graduation rate of the top three college men's basketball programs in the country, primarily made up of minority athletes, was 25 percent, 27 percent, and 29 percent, respectively.[11] Although the NCAA didn't provide these data, the athletes' graduation rate would in all likelihood have looked particularly bad if it had been compared to that of the other full scholarship students at the university.

Race aside, this poor graduation rate should not come as a surprise. If students, white or black, are given college scholarships on some other basis than academic excellence or academic potential—indeed, if these students are at or near the bottom of their high school classes in ability, commitment, and achievement—then it would be foolish to anticipate their attainment of academic success. In addition, if we factor in all the time and effort that these young people have to put into sports, and the fact that they may be counseled to take easy classes that do not count toward graduation so they can focus more attention on the crucial business of playing sports and staying eligible, then these extremely low graduation rates are even more understandable and predictable.

If sports is to be a true academic resource for minority athletes, it is not enough to put the blame on high schools and universities for not educating minority student-athletes, as has been the tendency. It isn't enough to increase pressure on coaches to make sure their players graduate. Most certainly high schools and colleges should be held responsible for the richness of the educational opportunities they provide minority and other athletes. But even as schools and coaches must be responsible *to* students and should be criticized if they aren't, it is a bad idea to hold them responsible *for* students. Students have to be responsible for themselves.

It is unrealistic to expect schools to carry people along who don't take personal responsibility for achieving success no matter what obstacles stand in their way. Education is not like surgery where the patient lies there and receives the benefits of the process. Education is something to pursue with all the personal resources one can muster. No matter how good the school, students won't learn or get good grades or graduate if they in effect simply stretch out on the operating table and wait for the doctors (teachers and professors and coaches) to do their jobs—or even worse, don't even come into the operating room (go to class).

Every individual who has been successful academically will tell you the way to do it: take challenging courses and programs, get to class, respect and support the person who's teaching you, and study with all you've got. If some kind of knowledge gap, how-to-study problem, or learning disability is holding you back, go to work with the best help available and fix it or learn how to compensate for it—get it out of the way. That is how to succeed in school. Anyone or anything that deflects students from that reality does them a disservice.

As well-intentioned as I know it is, it is bad psychology to tell students that the schools or coaches—or society, through social oppression or racism—are to blame for them not learning and achieving good grades. This gives students an excuse for failure, and when people have an excuse for failure, and particularly when it is a *good* excuse, it is human nature that more than a few will make use of it. An excuse doesn't pay the rent or build someone's skills or self-esteem. Having a high school diploma or a college degree is far better than the best of reasons for not having one. Also, if you tell young people that something outside of them is responsible for their success or lack of success in school, you are tacitly telling them that they do not have control of their own fate. If they get the idea that what really counts is what teachers and coaches do, that that is where the power is to make good things happen in school, the result is likely to be students who feel that they can't succeed academically unless and until these others allow them to—or, even more, *make* them—succeed. Students might get the idea that it isn't their fault that they are goofing off; think that it doesn't matter what they do; wait around for the situation to improve and flunk their classes in the meantime; or eventually get so frustrated, impatient, or hopeless that they drop out of school. The irony is that these same young people would never apply that attitude to their sport.

Although I care deeply about athletes who don't learn or graduate, I don't excuse them. I believe I help students most by believing in their capability to successfully meet the challenges they confront and by standing ready to do anything I can to support them as they take on these challenges with all that they have. But while I and other educators may be able to help some by taking on this attitude, it is the forces outside the school that can be most helpful—namely communities, families, intellectuals, journalists, religious leaders, politicians, and sports personalities. John Ogbu, an African-American sociologist, asserts: "The black community must reexamine its own perceptions and interpretations of school learning. Apparently, black children's general perception of academic pursuit as only 'acting white' is learned in the black community. Cultural or public recognition of those who are academically successful should be made a frequent event, as is generally done in the case of those who succeed in the fields of sports and entertainment."[12] Beyond this kind of recognition, everyone who has a forum and the respect of those who would hear the message needs to take up the cause of academic responsibility and excellence.

What has been learned and internalized can be replaced with new, more empowering thoughts and habits. And that doesn't have to mean playing down sports in deference to other pursuits. Rather, it can mean using sports as a positive example of the kind of self-reliance, dedication, perseverance, spirit, pride, and accomplishment that can characterize other involvements in life, including school-work. John Hoberman ends his book by saying that "the black ath-lete's tragedy is that he can neither advance nor lead his race in the modern world."[13] I disagree. The finest black athletes represent a standard for what engagement with the world is like at its very best. That exemplification can advance us all.

The challenge for you and your children is to make use of the posi-tive attributes of sports and to avoid its negative ones. One of the ways to do that is to learn from the examples of others. This chapter on social class is a good place to examine how the upper classes tend to approach sports. My assumption is that they know something about how things work in this society. They have been able to secure and maintain power and status, and they know how to provide for themselves materially.

How do the upper classes approach sports? They play sports avid-ly, intensely. They use sports to build competitiveness in their children. They see sports as recreation and a way to build skills and make social contacts. They focus on lifetime sports such as golf, tennis, and sailing. They see sports as part of what a well-rounded person does. But they don't use sports to build an identity. They don't let sports consume them, and they are careful not to let athletics get in the way of doing what it takes to live well in later life. They don't kid themselves into thinking that sports is the way they are going to make it in America. It's up to you and your children to decide how to incorporate sports into your lives, but it wouldn't hurt to reflect for a time on this orientation. For what it is worth, personally I think it makes the most sense.

CHAPTER 8

What Makes Athletes Successful?

In light of the importance (at least as I see it) of achievement in sports if children do participate, parents need to examine what makes good athletes good. Why are some athletes better than others? How do good athletes approach their sport? How do they achieve top results? Why do some athletes reach their highest potential and others not? I explore these questions in this chapter for two major reasons. First, parents have to decide how much to encourage their children to participate in organized athletics. One factor to take into account when making that decision is whether a child has what it takes to be successful in sports. Comparing what their child is like to what successful athletes are like will help in that regard. Second, parents have to decide how best to support their child's success in sports if the child does get involved. Knowing how accomplished athletes engage their sport can guide parents in making that determination.

As I prepared this chapter on athletic excellence, I reflected on the fact that Ken Heise in his letter and in our conversation had not mentioned how well he thought his son and daughter were going to do in sports. He also had not talked about whether he envisioned them being average or top-flight performers. Nor did he say what he hoped for and would encourage and support in this area. Except for his one comment about Julie being good at shooting baskets, Ken's focus was on the positive personal changes in his children that he was certain would come from a sports experience: increased levels of physical activity, decreased boredom, strengthened character, a better work ethic, greater motivation to succeed, heightened confidence, and a toughening up or masculinization for his son, David.

Although Ken's children are quite young and not involved in organized sports at this point, Ken's perspective probably will change as they get older and participate in organized athletics. My guess is that if Julie and David become involved in sports, Ken is going to be at the games rooting for them to excel—not just to participate, but to excel. I'll bet that when he is sitting in the stands, and at other times too, he will start imagining his kids hitting home runs and scoring touchdowns and sinking the winning basket at the buzzer and being carried off the field on their teammates' shoulders. Perhaps he is even having fleeting fantasies along these lines now.

This is to be expected: it is human nature to want your children to do well in any activity they take on. More than that, it makes rational sense to want them to do well. Why? For one thing, even if you just want them to have some fun playing sports, as a practical matter it is almost always more enjoyable for a child if he or she is successful at the activity. Success feels good; it's more fun. That goes for the parents attending the game too. It can be demoralizing watching shots whizzing by the hockey goaltender you brought into the world. Five or six bearhug celebrations by the other team while your one-and-only digs the puck out of the net with his head down can dampen your enjoyment.

The same analysis applies if you regard sports as a place for your children to make friends. Even though your feelings toward your children won't change no matter how they do in sports (I hope this is true, anyway), I'm afraid the rest of the world tends to be friendlier to stars than it is to benchwarmers.

Your feeling that there is something important at stake in your children's accomplishments in sports is justified on developmental grounds as well. In Chapter 2 I made the point that central to childhood and adolescence is the resolution for better or worse of issues related to (among others) personal capability and worth, self-respect, character, and individual identity. To successfully handle these challenges, it is vitally important that children live their lives with effectiveness. The greater the significance children attribute to their participation in sports, the more of themselves they give to sports, the more time and energy they devote to sports, the more important it is that they achieve at least a fair amount of success on the terms established by the particular sport they play and the specific sports situation in which they play it. Athletes can explain away or compensate for failure—by being the team funny guy or nice guy or deferring guy, for example—but it still grinds them down. No matter what you want out of a sports experience for your child, you need to take achievement level into account.

To organize this discussion of individual achievement in sports (I won't be talking about team success), I have divided the material into physical, characterological, and mental categories. As you read, keep in mind that what supports accomplishment in sports may also support accomplishment in other areas of life as well. Look for ways by which what is said here can be generalized and applied to education, business, social relationships, and other areas—I think much of it can.

PHYSICAL FACTORS

I start with the factor that plays by far the greatest role in producing high levels of accomplishment in sports. Physical talent is certainly not the only thing that makes a good athlete, but it is by a long shot the biggest factor, and we kid ourselves if we think otherwise. Many people, including parents and young athletes themselves, operate from the premise that what really counts is how much you want to succeed at sports and how much time and effort you put into the activity, how much practice and so on. Although desire and hard work count a great deal—and I will explore their importance later in this chapter—nothing matters as much as ability, God-given talent.

Many feel uncomfortable talking about differences in innate ability. Perhaps their beliefs about equality of opportunity or individual rights have led them to an assumption of equality of capability; or perhaps they subscribe to the view that differences in capability are insignificant in the scheme of things. In truth, although individuals are equal in their fundamental worth as human beings and in their rights before the law, they differ in every way imaginable, including athletic talent.

A confirmation of the limits that talent imposes may not sit well with many people. The notion that everyone can do the job if given the chance and works hard enough is a comforting one, and a useful one when it leads us to strive hard toward an attainable goal we would not shoot for otherwise. Ultimately, however, we serve ourselves best when we accept that we have strengths and weaknesses—I mean the real ones, not the ones we falsely assume we have or those that others falsely tell us we have—and then play to our strengths. That is a lesson I would like young people to learn.

At the pre-university level, most top athletes are good at a number of sports. It is common for the star football player to also be a hockey and track standout, for example. No matter what sport some young people try, it seems, they are good at it. In fact, one way to spot a good young athlete is this across-the-board capability. It is an indication of basic athletic talent.

Whereas superior general athletic talent allows youths to be good all-around athletes, as they get older and involved in higher levels of competition, the unique requirements of particular sports make it difficult for them to be stars in more than one sport. At the elite level, if an athlete is proficient in one sport, he or she is unlikely to be even near that same level in another. At the high school level, an 82-mile-an-hour fastball will blow hitters away, but even in the low minor leagues it will get you a quick shower. In pro football, cornerbacks—the players who defend against the opposing team's pass receivers—have to be able to run forty yards in 4.4 or 4.5 seconds. That is not just fast; that is *blazing* fast. Tennis players must be extremely quick and possess remarkable hand-and-eye coordination. Basketball players must have great agility and, usually, height way above the norm. John Stockton, an all-star guard in the NBA for years, is an unremarkable-looking person, that is, until you check out his hands—they are enormous. His huge hands give him a great advantage when handling the basketball.

In recent years Bo Jackson, Deion Sanders, and Brian Jordan have played outstandingly at the professional level in both football and baseball. But these great athletes are among very few who cross over from one sport to another at the top level. By far the more typical case is Michael Jordan, arguably the greatest basketball player who has ever lived. When Jordan applied his immense work ethic and competitiveness to professional baseball, even with the best of instruction the result was around a .200 batting average in AA baseball, a league two notches below the major leagues.

One day Jordan was in a crouch taking pitches at the start of an inning while the regular catcher was putting on his gear. As Jordan was getting up out of his catcher's squat, another player laughed and remarked that it looked like a giraffe trying to get up. He was saying this about the most graceful basketball player I have ever seen. In one sport, a ballet dancer; in another, a giraffe.

It is true that Jordan tried baseball at the advanced age of 31, and perhaps he would have made the majors if he had started at 18 or 20. He was a fine baseball player as a youngster growing up, winning a North Carolina player-of-the-year award at twelve. Nevertheless, if he had played baseball from the beginning—or golf, a sport he loves and devotes a great deal of time to—he would never have become anything approaching the superstar he became in basketball. All his wonderful personal qualities would have been there in baseball and golf, and they would have served him well, but the physical talent simply isn't there in those sports; and it has to be, that is the point.

Most often, true athletic talent shows itself early. I remember reading glowing reports about Wayne Gretzky—who turned out to be as good a pro hockey player as ever lived—when he was 12-years-old. It was clear to everyone who saw him at age 12 how special a player Wayne was going to be. Parents should not hold on to the idea that even though their children are not very good at a sport now, they will likely improve greatly later on. In my experience, it rarely works that way. Far more often, it is as these Olympic swimmers describe: "As soon as I hit the water, I was good. I could get in the pool and beat anybody." "I started winning in my age group real quickly. That's how I started getting positive reinforcement right from the start." "I was really successful at the age-group meets [8 and under]. I won a lot of first places."[1] And from a parent: "She was beautiful. . . . She was immediately a good swimmer. She was a winner from the start, which made it easy for us to be enthusiastic."[2]

It is true that if they work hard enough most children can become halfway good at something they really aren't cut out to do. As a practical matter, most youngsters can reach mediocrity in a sport, or even become fairly proficient, if they are willing to pay the price in time and effort. But becoming a truly excellent athlete is something else again. That takes not only dedication and hard work, it takes talent. Life flows so much easier when you put your energies into what you are naturally good at doing.

It is simply not realistic to think you can rise above your talent level. My experience has been that by and large stars stay stars and average players stay average—we stay in our slots. If you work hard you will get better than you are, but you will still stay in your particular rank. We like to think that isn't the case, and we make much of what appear to be instances of players coming from way back to become star performers. That does happen every now and again, but most often when an individual suddenly becomes a star it is a matter of that person growing in size to a point at which his or her ability can show itself, or he gets some handicap out of his way such as excess weight, insufficient strength, or bad habits. In the vast majority of these instances, coaches who know these athletes will tell you that their ability was apparent even before the athletes shot ahead.

In some ways it is helpful if so-so players think that greater dedication and effort will transform them into superior players. From the coaches' perspective this is a good deal, because if players accept this idea they will increase their commitment and effort, with the result that even if they don't become top performers the coach will still get the most that is possible out of them. And from the players' perceptive it is positive too, because they will have gotten the most out of their athletic talent. All the same, to the degree that the athletes thought they were going to step up into a totally new category of player, they were operating under a delusion, and it leaves open the question of whether they might not have been better off putting their efforts into something where they had greater potential for success—fiction writing or competitive bridge, for example.

Most people can pick out good athletes even if they don't know much about the particular sport involved. At least they can when it isn't their child they are assessing. Recently, I went to a youth soccer game, and even though I don't know much about soccer, I could immediately identify the best players. It wasn't hard. Grace, speed, agility, coordination, and quickness jump out at you. You may not know how much ability your child has, and your child may not know, but others do. They won't necessarily tell you, however, because that wouldn't be polite. They may even tell you false or misleading things they believe you want to hear.

It isn't easy for children and their parents to be objective when evaluating the children's innate talent. There is an understandable tendency to overestimate the children's capacity and potential. However, for people who value being good at something, it is imperative that they be realistic about the natural ability they or those they care about bring to any enterprise. The danger is that children will try to become something that God or nature never intended them to be. They might spend their childhoods struggling along a path that leads toward a destination that is too far away to ever reach, and in the process never catch sight of their own natural path that lies unnoticed off to the side.

If your child just wants to participate in sports to have some enjoyment and excitement and be with other kids, then this discussion doesn't matter much. But if your child is starting to take sports seriously—or you are—and being really good at sports is what they are aiming for or what you want, then it is important to take talent into consideration with as much objectivity as you can, and help your child do the same. Perhaps one of your children's coaches can help you and your child make an accurate, objective assessment of your child's athletic talent.

CHARACTEROLOGICAL FACTORS

Now to a second category: characterological, or personal, factors and their relationship to athletic success. That is to say, factors related to personality, individual makeup, style, patterns of adaptation, approach to life, character—the terms applied to this area vary. It comes down to what the person is made of and how he or she approaches life.

As we know, talent alone does not ensure accomplishment. We can all think of people who never produce to a level commensurate with their abilities. If you look into why they don't, very often you find that it is because something about them is not as developed as it needs to be, or they have a personal flaw or deficit of some kind. Saying this is not to put them down; it is but to state a fact about them.

What are the personal qualities or character traits that support achievement in sports? When pressed to point to the differences between Olympic swimmers and their peers who didn't make it that far, parents talked about their "incredible independence, determination, and competitiveness."[3] A study of elite tennis players found that these athletes believed they possessed personal qualities that were as important—if not more important—than their physical characteristics. One tennis player said this about himself as a child:

I was a fighter. I'd never give up. That's one thing, I was an excellent competitor. I couldn't stand to lose. If they had to drag me off the court, I'd stay out there and do whatever I had to do to win the match. If that meant staying out there five hours, I'd stay out there on the court for five hours to win the match. I was really determined. Plus I practiced twice as hard as anyone else. I used to just go out and play for hours and hours. And I used to feel that I had to do that to make up for some of the lack of physical size. So my competitiveness and my willingness to work hard have always been the two biggest things that have gotten me as far as I have, I think.

Another tennis player said: "I was competitive. I know my coaches liked my temperament. I didn't get upset too fast, and they say that I worked hard." And still another player: "People noticed that I worked hard. That I practiced hard. That probably even intimidated some of them. . . . [Also] I was a highly competitive person." A parent about his daughter: "She is a fighter. She doesn't give up and she can get way down in a match and come back."[4] I think you can see the pattern in these responses.

The study of tennis players just quoted was part of a larger study of accomplished individuals and their parents to ascertain what others might learn from their experience. The researchers studied achievers in music, art, mathematics, and science as well as athletics. The principal investigator concluded that the three personal qualities most related to the realization of an individual's talent were a strong interest and emotional commitment to a particular field; a desire to reach a high level of attainment in that field; and a willingness to put in the great amounts of time and effort needed to reach these very high levels of achievement in that field.[5] If your child possesses these qualities in relation to some sport, it greatly increases the chances he or she will make maximum use of his or her talent in that context.

The strong emotional commitment high achievers display needs to be underscored. Fine athletes are capable of *intense* commitment. These individuals can rise above dabbling. They can say YES to a sport, and *really* involve themselves in it. Many people never reach a complete YES in anything in their lives. They exist somewhere between YES and NO in everything they do. They put a bit less than all they have into the activity or task. They go a bit less than all out.

I was once on a softball team that included an NHL hockey player. Never in all the years I played athletics have I ever been around anyone with that level of engagement in a sport, and this was just a summer softball league! When he played, he PLAYED. His mode of participation in that activity was grounded in a commitment to the others on the team, but that was just part of it, and I don't think it was the biggest part. The biggest part was his commitment to himself. He mattered to himself. He took his own life seriously. If he was going to take the time to play on a softball team, he was going to really do it, not merely do it. This player has since retired from hockey and has gone into business, where he has also been highly successful. After being around him that summer, I think I know one of the major reasons why.

MENTAL FACTORS

Now to a third category of factors that account for athletic excellence: the mental side of sports. Time and again, top athletes affirm that mastering the mental aspects of their sport is crucial. I agree, and this is especially the case at the highest levels of competition where the difference in the abilities of the athletes is so slight.

Mental Ability

Researchers have postulated that superior athletes often have a faster than normal information-processing and response time. This means that some athletes can recognize a stimulus sooner, have a wider variety of response possibilities stored in their brains, and can initiate movement commands to themselves more quickly than others can.[6]

I think of Dan Marino, a great quarterback for so many years with the Miami Dolphins. Marino was an All-American quarterback in college at the University of Pittsburgh. Nevertheless, in the pro draft several other quarterbacks were selected ahead of him. I understand that one of the reasons that Dan was not drafted more quickly was that he scored quite low on a general intelligence test the NFL gives to potential players. There was some question about whether he was bright enough to handle the complexities of quarterbacking a pro offense.

Soon after Dan reported to the Dolphins' training camp, the coaches saw that he possessed a wonderful mental ability that had not shown up on the intelligence test. It was a lightning-quick recognition-and-appropriate-response time. Miami head coach Don Shula said Dan could spot a receiver breaking free and throw the right pass faster than anyone he had ever seen. In a way the Dolphins had lucked out. They had gotten something they hadn't thought to look for. This example highlights the shallowness of thinking about mental capability. We tend to see mental ability, or intelligence, as a unitary phenomenon, and we measure it with a single number, an IQ. Psychologists, on the other hand, are finding that there are actually many facets to intelligence and they are identifying kinds of intelligence the general public has not taken note of. Yale psychologist Robert Sternberg describes three kinds of intelligence: one that promotes analytical and critical thinking; one that leads to the development of new and creative ideas; and one that enables individuals to respond quickly and productively to everyday events and experiences (Marino's kind?).[7] Harvard psychologist Howard Gardner has proposed a theory of multiple intelligences including logical-mathematical, visual-spatial, bodily-kinesthetic (Marino?), and several personal intelligences (the ability to understand other people and one's own inner workings).[8]

Thus, it isn't that Marino was dumb, but rather that he was smart in a different way than the test measured. Painters, chess champions, writers, psychologists, entrepreneurs, architects, carpenters, and athletes undoubtedly each have mental strengths that contribute to their success at what they do. But we will miss that fact if we persist in thinking about intelligence in the traditionally narrow way.

Mental Outlook

In addition to the mental abilities that individuals bring to their participation in sports, there is also their mental outlook—their perspective or orientation, the way they view their involvement in the sport.

Scholars and researchers note two basic orientations in athletes. The specific terms these writers use to describe the two vary, but I will refer to them as an *ego orientation* and a *task orientation*.[9] Although both orientations motivate athletes to perform well, sports research has shown that a task orientation has more to recommend it than an ego orientation.

Basically, an ego orientation is at work when you participate in sports to puff yourself up. You play ball to get attention and affirmation or to make a point about your worth. Ironically, the ego orientation is very much centered in other people, because the ego is served by referencing your performance to others' opinion of you. Other people have power over you, since they are the ones to make the crucial decision of how well you stack up.

An ego orientation can take three basic forms.[10] Athletes may operate in one of the three forms, or they may be guided by a combination of two, or all three. They can also mix in the task perspective, which I will describe next. This isn't anything out of the ordinary; people are often characterized by multiple motivations, including contrasting and contradicting motives that pull them this way and that.

One form of ego orientation is to play sports to win social approval. The idea is to look as if you have virtuous intentions, a strong commitment, and/or that you do well at this sport activity, and that thereby you deserve the approval or admiration of teammates, spectators, and parents. A social approval frame of reference often centers on demonstrating one's effort to others. When playing sports, young children may especially be trying to please a parent or some other adult and win their approval. Parents can generally motivate young children by attributing hard effort to their involvement in sports—or anything else—by letting them know that what they are doing pleases them: "I can see you are trying very hard. I really like that. Good for you!"

A second form that the ego-oriented perspective can take among athletes is to play sports in order to demonstrate ability. In this case the contest is a challenge and opportunity for athletes to maintain or enhance other people's favorable impression of their talent. They want to hear, "That person is really good!"

A third form of ego orientation is when athletes seek to demonstrate superiority. In this instance, sports is a way to show you are better than the other guy. Sports is a means of establishing higher status. Your performance beats that of other players, and therefore you deserve to be ranked above them. You are playing the sport to make that point.

In contrast to an ego orientation, a task orientation is at work when an athlete sees sports as a context in which to get a job done. With this approach, the athlete assesses success on the basis of the quality of the work itself and not on the responses of observers. The criterion for determining quality can be a normative standard, an objective standard inherent in the game itself, or the athlete's own individual standard.

An example of a normative standard is hitting over .300 in baseball, a level of batting excellence established over time by the performances of the best players.

An example of an objective standard is to "play against the game," a phrase I associate with University of Indiana basketball coach Bob Knight. When Knight speaks of playing against the game, he means the attempt by the players on his team to play basketball as it is ideally played. When they operate from this frame, the Indiana players are not so much in competition against an opponent as they are, as it were, playing against the game of basketball itself. How well can they pass and shoot and rebound and play defense in relation to the finest form of those activities?

An example of an individual standard would be if the best a basketball player has ever done is average five rebounds a game, and now she increases her average to seven. In this case, the athlete has gone beyond the level of excellence she had established up this point.

Operating from a task orientation, the athlete sees the athletic event primarily as an opportunity to learn about the game and success and oneself. It is a chance to get better. It is an occasion to solve problems, seek mastery, and improve one's craft. Research over the last decade indicates that a task orientation is the best route for an athlete. Studies have shown that a task orientation results in a stronger work ethic, greater persistence, and optimal performance given the capabilities of the individual. A task approach has been found to lead to the choice of strategies that will maximize performance levels and personal satisfaction. Individual studies have linked a task strategy to the following positive outcomes:

- higher levels of sports interest and enjoyment, and lower levels of boredom
- greater learning about the sport
- more frequent participation
- a belief in fitness, skill development, collaboration with others, and trying things one can't do
- stronger social relationships with other children
- maintaining one's concentration and feeling good about the game
- being less worried about one's performance
- being less likely to perceive cheating as legitimate

Interestingly enough, a task orientation most often creates greater social approval, which is evidence that a task approach may well be a better way to accomplish the ends sought by an ego orientation. Additionally, teams with higher winning percentages were found to be less ego-involved than those who weren't as successful.[11]

Although ego-involved athletes are often very highly motivated to get involved in sports and to perform well, they have so much on the line personally that they are quite fragile and tend to tighten up and fail to do their best in the game. When things don't go well for them, they may increase their effort but fail to employ the best strategies to improve their play. Or they might go in the opposite direction and reduce their effort and claim a lack of interest, or drop out as a way to reduce the threat to themselves and save face. Ironically, athletes with an ego orientation may invoke "helpless" behavior patterns and exhibit low persistence as a way of avoiding a threatening challenge. It is not surprising that with so much at stake personally, ego-oriented athletes have been shown in the research to experience greater stress and to be less likely to emphasize team membership and affiliation. It should also not be surprising to learn that ego-involved athletes place less emphasis on fairness, more frequently endorse aggression, and are more likely to do whatever it takes to come out on top regardless of how fair it is.[12]

Successful people in all walks of life, including sports, bring a *positive mental attitude* to their endeavors. They don't dwell on what is wrong at the expense of what is right, or why something can't or won't get done in the future. Their style is to focus on what is worth accomplishing, and then put their energies into making it happen. They are grounded in hope, not despair.

In a study of swimmers, those with a pessimistic style—the tendency to see themselves, situations, and the future in a negative light—had a significantly higher number of poor swims relative to their capability than those who had a more optimistic mode of interpreting events. The researchers noted that negativity in swimmers was not a function of talent; pessimism was as prevalent in high-level swimmers as low-level swimmers. The second part of this study sought to determine how athletes' style influences their ability to bounce back after something bad happens to them. Results indicated that the optimists tended to do at least as well on the next swim after a failure, whereas the pessimists tended to do worse.[13] It appears that optimistic athletes can better handle the many "mini-failures" that are inevitable in athletics.

It is likely that athletes who perform better under pressure have more positive thoughts than other athletes.[14] Among these positive thoughts are what researchers term *self-enhancing affirmations*. These athletes say positive things to themselves ("Nice job of working the count on the pitcher last time"), and they stay away from negative self-talk ("I bet I kick the next grounder"). When negative self-talk pops into their heads, they immediately counter it: "I've made two good plays in this game in addition to the one I messed up. If the ball is hit to me, I'll handle it cleanly." Successful athletes also use *positive imagery*. They imagine doing something right rather than creating inner pictures of what has gone wrong or might go wrong in the future.

Research indicates that top athletes report lower amounts of anxiety both prior to and during competition. That could have to do with the fact that whereas some athletes view the tension before a big game as a likely harbinger of bad times, others interpret this arousal as exciting, challenging, motivating, and personally beneficial. This second group reports feeling "juiced" or "pumped" or "psyched." Same event for both groups, but very different attributions of meaning, which lead to very different emotional, and, in all likelihood, behavioral responses. This is another illustration of the importance of having a positive mental perspective.

Even though successful athletes are positive, their heads are most certainly not in the clouds. They are very *rational* in their approach to their sport. They see the sport circumstance and their own performance as something that can be understood and controlled. They don't assume that whatever happens to them is due to external, unstable, or unfathomable forces. They don't just try a little harder or hope to have a good game next time. They use their minds to ensure good games. They analyze themselves, their thoughts, their actions, and their circumstances and, based on that analysis, they devise ways to improve their performance.[15]

Good athletes think deeply about their involvement in their sport and are highly insightful about it. Studies have shown that top-flight athletes concentrate harder on their specific goals and movements and are better at designing coping strategies for dealing with poor performances.[16] It is very important for young children, even before they are old enough to do it well, to come to value making sense of things: *What is going on? Why is this happening? What will improve things?* Youngsters need to learn that sports success involves hard thinking.

Good athletes can *concentrate*. You hear athletes talk time and again about the need to focus. Researchers use the term *attention control* to describe the process of giving one's complete attention for as long as necessary to the task at hand to the exclusion of everything extraneous. It is a skill worth developing, and for many people it is hard to develop in a world that encourages them to constantly shift and divide their attention. Every sports practice and game is an opportunity to work on one's ability to concentrate.

Research shows good athletes to be *self-confident*.[17] Undoubtedly their confidence is to some extent a byproduct of their previous successes: if things have gone well for you in the past, you are more likely to assume they will go well in the future. To the degree that this is true, it further underscores the importance of successful experiences for children. It is difficult to build confidence on a foundation of failures. With that said, however, it can't be assumed that confidence is simply a one-to-one reflection of past performance. Anyone who has been around sports will tell you they have known some highly talented athletes who were not nearly as confident as one would expect them to be. They will also tell you that this held these athletes back.

Arnold Schwarzenegger has said that one key factor in his success in bodybuilding, business, and films is his confidence. He speaks of confidence as if it is a choice he has made for himself. To the degree that confidence can be chosen, it appears certain that it is in one's interest to do so.

Good athletes learn from *observing the best*. Good athletes make it a point to watch and analyze the ways the top athletes think and behave, and then they use what they have learned to improve their own athletic capability and achievement. An interesting piece of research involving basketball free-throw shooting demonstrates the advantages of modeling and positive imagery. A combination of watching a good free-throw shooter and imagining themselves shooting with good form and success—without actually practicing—significantly increased players' free-throw shooting proficiency.[18] It is very important for young athletes to be around good models—people doing things the right way—and attend to how these superior performers achieve success and then try it that way themselves.

Lawrence Harrison's book, *Who Prospers?* asks the question: What accounts for economic and social success?[19] Harrison's investigations show that it isn't where you come from, what color you are, who you know, or any of those other things people usually list. Rather, it is what you believe in, what you stand for—that is what really matters. More than anything, success has to do with *values*. Harrison's study wasn't about athletes, but it applies to sports success. What strikes me about those that are successful in every area of life, including sports, is that they have achievement-oriented values. Their fundamental convictions center around learning, growth, and accomplishment. These individuals more than simply prefer to achieve or hope to achieve, they *intend* to achieve. They are committed to doing what needs to be done now in order to be productive in the future. They believe in self-discipline, hard work, perseverance, and the rigorous use of their minds. And they prosper while others languish.

A PROMISING APPROACH TO SPORTS

This is speculative, but I have the sense that there are three basic ways of involving oneself in sports that contribute to maximizing athletic performance. It seems to me that the use of all three in the combination that best fits a particular athlete and a particular sports situation is the best approach for young athletes to adopt when they are physically and developmentally mature enough to do so. Because it is multi-faceted and emphasizes a reflective engagement in sports, the combined approach I will outline appears most suited to teenagers and adults. This orientation is best viewed as a direction in which children should move as they become older and increasingly involved in organized sports. When children are very young—before 12 or so—it is enough, I believe, that they taste a bit of the variety of possibilities sports offers, get in some physical activity, be part of a social occasion and have fun, acquire some very basic technical skills, and learn to respond to coaching.

Sports as Self-Expression

The first dimension of the approach I see as promising for maturing athletes—after 11 or 12, let's say, and increasingly as they get older—is to look upon sports competition as an opportunity for *self-expression*.

To illustrate, consider the enormous contribution African Americans have made to the sport of basketball. Blacks have literally taken the game to new heights—basketball soars today when it once had its feet firmly planted on the floor. If you remember or have seen films of the old two-hand set shot, you know what I mean. The grace and artistry that black basketball players have brought to the game is beautiful to behold. I am generalizing, but I believe this advance in the level of play is due in good part to the fact that black athletes—even very young ones—view basketball as a vehicle for expressing themselves. That is, they are not just there to compete and win. They play basketball as a means of personal and cultural expression.

Black players—well, all players now—speak of their "game." They are referring to their unique, individual styles of playing basketball, the aspects of the sport they emphasize, and their particular strengths as players. For the individual player, competition on the court is a chance to express his game, reveal who he is as a player at this point in his development. This may appear to be an ego orientation, but it isn't really. It is a *self* orientation; it reveals or shows the self. It is akin to an artist painting a picture. Probably the artist cares whether the viewer considers him talented and likes his work, but that isn't what motivated him to paint a particular picture. He painted it to express his being, his individuality. Similarly, there are many among the best basketball players who don't play their games primarily to show off their ability, to establish that they are better than someone else, or to win acceptance. Rather, these athletes are making it known, to themselves as much as anyone, who they are, what they represent, and how far they have come. Being who they are is a tre-mendously rewarding experience for these players, apart from any other reward it might bring. Playing in this way is an expression of the gifts of existence and mind and volition. It marks the presence of a never-before-and-never-again-replicated human being. It speaks to the joy of life.

A self-expressive posture contributes to excellence because the youngster is constantly seeking to improve himself or herself in order to make his or her expressions better and truer. It is a fas-cinating quest—especially for a teenager—to discover one's nature and one's possibilities. With this frame of reference, the athlete is more likely to remain focused and not be nervous and tighten up, because even though he is aware that there are spectators he is grounded primarily in the process of bringing out what is inside him. The sports performance is thus on the order of a jazz performance. One's individuality is expressed and at the same time blended with the other players' performances, with less attention and concern being paid to the responses of those who are observing.

Sports as a Chance to Learn and Develop

A young person can view sports as an opportunity to *learn and de-velop*. In this case, competition is a means to learn about the sport and yourself, about other players, and about team success. It is a means to become better than you are now. Whereas the self-expres-sive manner of engagement was fundamentally focused on revealing oneself, this one is focused on developing oneself. The result is the creation not only of very good players, but also the enhancement of the team and the sport generally, as the player learns from his exper-ience and then applies it to his play and takes himself and the game to new levels. I believe this learning-and-growth perspective will keep the athlete more grounded and avoid the fragility that goes along with ego-based involvement.

Sports as a Contribution to Others and the Team

The athlete can participate in sports in order to *contribute to others and the team*. Operating from this frame, his intention is to support his teammates' development as players and to help them play their best in the game. If it is a team sport, he seeks to help his team perform to the best of its capability and, with good sportsmanship, to win. Superior athletes do not just play for themselves. The mark of truly fine players is that they make everyone around them better. They expect and demand the best from the other players, and they contribute to bringing it about.

The best athletes integrate the perspectives just described. At the same time that they are concerned with expressing their individual way of playing in its highest, most evolved form, they are also using the competition to learn and develop as players, and they are contributing to the success of other athletes and the team. This integration is not always easy. Good athletes often have to deal with tensions among the three dimensions of this overall approach. For instance, there may be occasions when basketball players feel compelled to sacrifice their game, their style of play, and perhaps their own development as a player in deference to the interests of others or the team. There are many laudable examples of fine basketball players suppressing their offensive moves in order to get other players more involved in the flow, or playing out of position because that best serves the needs of the team.

A grasp of these three perspectives can shed light on some of the conflicts between coaches and players. Coaches are most often oriented toward the team; that is their predominant frame of reference. Coaches' success and reputation, and sometimes their future employment, is linked to the team performing well and winning games. For better or worse, every leader—whether it be a coach, politician, or chief executive officer—is going to sell the group as the most valued entity over the individual, and loyalty and service to the group as the worthiest conduct anyone can exhibit. The collective is the leader's responsibility, and it is the basis of the leader's rewards. When the group is the focus, the leader is the focus. When the group does well, the leader does well.

Thus, coaches' place in the scheme of things leads them to uphold team play and winning as the heart of the sports enterprise. Accordingly, they may talk about how the needs of the team transcend those of any individual player. They may come down hard on a player who thinks the game is about the experience of playing and trying out things and learning and having fun, condemning this attitude as selfish or not serious. In team sports especially, individual athletes have the job of balancing their goals and needs with the pressure to be good soldiers, as it were. The best athletes find a way to do it.

As I offer this expression-development-contribution triad, I don't want to appear to be saying that this approach best directs the attainment of athletic excellence in every case. People and situations are too variable for any generalization or strategy to be universally applicable. No doubt there are a number of superb athletes who are motivated by the desire to show the world they are the best or to get to the top. There are fine athletes who are driven to achieve by what isn't right in their lives. Many athletes use the competition of other athletes to push them forward in their sport. Nonetheless, I find this three-part approach to involvement in sports a useful way to look at things.

CONCLUSION

For a parent, it all comes down to the question of how good an athlete your child must be to be good enough.

Drawing on the discussion in Chapter 2, at any level of competition, your child ought to be good enough to support reasonable success relative to the standards of a particular sports situation. What is necessary to become a college or professional player? Of course, there are very few Michael Jordans and Wayne Gretzkys. You don't want to discourage children who don't show the early promise of a Wayne Gretzky or Michael Jordan. If everyone did that, there wouldn't be enough players in the country to field a team, much less a league. (Believe it or not, Jordan was cut from his high school basketball team his first year.) The question parents realistically need to resolve is this: Does my child have enough talent and enough of the requisite personal qualities to eventually become a competent college or pro athlete—successful, capable of having a good career, but not a star or hall-of-famer. A good initial sign to look for is that your child is among the very best at his or her current level of competition. It is probably safe to say that as an athlete ascends the pyramid of sport, top-of-the-line achievement is the minimum standard for having a reasonable hope of playing well at the next level. (Eventually, Jordan was a great high school basketball player.) The hope may not pan out, of course—we can think of superb high school and college athletes who discovered at the next level of play that the other players were better. When athletes are no longer stand-out excellent, then in all likelihood they have reached the ceiling of their advancement. It appears the best thing you can do is monitor your child's progress one level at a time, watching for signals of whether it is advisable for your child to keep climbing the pyramid—and to encourage your child to do the same.

I hope this discussion has given a clearer picture of what good athletes are like and the direction in which your child needs to move in order to become a more successful athlete. We'll build upon this material in the next chapter, which explores what you can do to support your child in achieving greater success and satisfaction in sports. I hope, too, that the material in this chapter has gotten you interested in the issue of achievement, and not just achievement in sports. Why are some people successful and others not? If you want to study this topic further, there are some good books on the subject.[20] Also, you can observe and learn as you go through your day-to-day activities. Personally, I find achievement a fascinating topic because it gets at the heart of a fundamental concern: the quality of what we create in the time we have available to us on this earth.

One last point: we shouldn't lose sight of the place of opportunity and encouragement in athletic achievement. One can have all the physical, personal, and mental equipment in the world, but if one isn't allowed to play, nothing will come of it. We need to make sure our society offers everyone a chance to develop their skills, invites everyone to try out for the team, and gives the positions to the ones who play them best.

CHAPTER 9

Parenting a Child in Sports

What can Ken and Melissa Heise, and you and other parents, do to support your children in having the best possible experience in organized sports? I think we have enough background and information now to address that question in this chapter, and at the same time tie together concepts and arguments contained in the previous chapters.

A basic premise guiding this discussion is that parenting in sports is not separate and distinct but rather just one aspect of the overall parenting responsibility, and that it must done with the larger context in mind. You parent in sports the same way you parent in other areas, and for the same reasons: to help your children have rich and happy childhoods; to help them become healthy, decent, and capable individuals ready to forge satisfying and productive adult lives; and to create loving and rewarding relationships with them that will last for a lifetime. Thus, I will first discuss good parenting in general and then how parenting in sports fits into that.

In the end, how much you promote sports in your child's life is a judgment you will have to make. What you do about sports depends on the effect sports has on the quality of your child's life, and on the quality of your own life. I can imagine a good life for a child with sports, and I can imagine an equally good life for a child without sports. I see nothing either in my experience or my research that makes sports an imperative activity. It comes down to how much a particular sports activity suits a child's personality, talents, and interests, and whether—or how much—it contributes to sound development in all its dimensions, to academic growth and success, and to good family relationships. As a parent of your particular child, you will have to weigh both the pluses and minuses of sports in your child's life.

THE SIX-MESSAGE FOUNDATION FOR GOOD PARENTING

I propose that there are six messages sent by a parent and received by a child that constitute the foundation for good parenting. They create a solid base from which parents can operate in every dimension of their relationship with their children, whether it is in home life, school, sports, or any other area. These six essential parent-to-child messages encourage the child to engage life fully. They motivate the child to do what will bring him or her personal happiness and satisfaction, and to successfully confront the challenges he or she faces.

This is not a list of techniques parents memorize and employ, and it is definitely not a one-shot deal—a five-minute speech or a single action. These six messages must be consistently conveyed over time. They are the sum total of many occasions and exchanges.

Messages can sometimes be missed or misinterpreted by children. Parents must be sensitive to that fact and be persistent in trying to get the messages across in such ways that children will take them in without blocking or distorting them. With that said, however, it is fair to assume that most of the time children pick up quite accurately the messages parents send out. If you send it through what you say and do, they will get it.

The Six Messages of Good Parenting

1. *I love you, and you will never lose my love.* I'm your mother (or father) and you are my daughter (or son), and I love you. That won't ever change, no matter what.

2. *You matter.* You count greatly. You are wanted. You belong here, you have a place here—with me, with the family, in the world. You have worth. You deserve love and respect and support. You are important—no one is more important than you are. What you think and do in your life is of utmost significance.

3. *You are special.* You are a unique and independent individual. You are distinctive. There has never been anyone like you, and there will never again be anyone like you, and that is glorious. Your life is your own. I want you to be who you are at your very best—that would be wonderful.

4. *I care deeply about you.* I am interested in you. I attend closely to you. I support you.

5. *I expect a lot of you, both now and in the future.* I believe in you. I think you can do it. I think you will do it. I have faith in you.

6. *You can trust and depend on me completely.* I am a solid person. You have in me a parent who is healthy, grounded, and stable. You are safe with me. I won't hurt you. I am here with you. I'll never abandon you.

Each of these six messages is positive in itself, and each complements the others and enhances their effect. If one of these six messages is absent in a child's life, it can vitiate or even eliminate the effect of the messages that are present. For example, children can get the message that their parents care about them but don't have high expectations for them. The message some parents communicate is, "I believe in you, but I am not going to attend to you very much and I am not going to be involved in what you are doing." In the way they conduct their lives, some parents are saying to their children, "I love you with all my heart, but you can't count on me because I am in turmoil in my own life."

Take a moment and think about these six messages in terms of your relationship to your child.

THE SIX PRINCIPLES OF PARENT IMPACT

If you want your child to develop personal responsibility or behave in a particular way, in sports or school or anywhere else, how do you go about getting it done? Establishing the six essential messages just described will increase your influence as a parent. But beyond that, I will outline six principles of parent impact. Put into practice, each of these principles enhances your ability to shape the direction of your child's life amid all the forces bidding for children's attention and nudging them this way and that. Used in combination with the six messages, these six principles compound the power you have to positively affect your children.

The Principles

1. *Clarify your priorities and commitments regarding your children.* If you are unclear or ambiguous about your goals and whether you really mean business you won't be as purposeful, focused, and powerful as you could be. It is important not to confuse purposefulness with being dogmatic. You can go directly toward something you want to accomplish and still be open to altering your direction if new insights and changed circumstances make it advisable.

In particular, you need to be very clear about your intentions relative to the childhood concerns that were the topics of earlier chapters: child and adolescent development (Chapter 2); academics (Chapters 3 and 5); personal character (Chapter 4); gender (Chapter 6); class and race (Chapter 7); and level of sports excellence (Chapter 8).

What are you going to foster in your child? Put it into words for yourself, or tell someone. Write it down. Imagine what it would look like if it actually happened. Imagine yourself contributing to it happening. Experience your convictions. Make them part of you. Make your convictions the energy that propels you moment by moment and directs your actions.

2. *Model what you value.* Don't just point the way to your children, *be* the way. Represent what you believe in for your children in the way you conduct your own life. If you believe in hard work or integrity or independence or personal development or decency, whatever it is, be an example of those things yourself. For better or worse, parents are very influential models for their children to emulate. Keep that in mind.

3. *Share your insights, priorities, and hopes with your children.* Tell them what you think about things. Share your convictions. You don't have to remain silent. You don't have to stay out of it. You don't have to hint about what you want from your children. If you believe something about the place of sports in life, or character, or school, say it.

Level with your child about where you stand. When you level, you aren't whining or scolding or beseeching or absolutely demanding anything. You aren't necessarily saying your child must do anything with what you have said. There are times when what you are leveling about is indeed a ruling about something, an edict to the child, and you are the one who has to determine when those times are based on your priorities and commitments. But probably in most cases you are simply letting your child know how you see things or what you prefer. You are communicating what is true for you and what is important to you. I am not talking about a long prepared speech or lecture, or anything formalized. It is a matter of being brief and to the point when the right occasion arises.

You may be told by some that children resent hearing these kinds of things or pay no attention to them. Children don't want to be nagged or ordered about by their parents (which means it is best to keep your edicts to a minimum), but they do want to hear from them. Children want to learn from their parents. However well-meant it may be, a parent saying "Anything you do is all right with me" is often heard by the child as "I don't care about you" or "You don't matter." I can't count the number of times young people have told me about something their mother or father said to them about school (or work or relationships or personal deportment or sports) that they took to heart and incorporated into their lives. The youngsters especially took to heart what their parent said—and here is how this all goes together—when it came from a parent who clearly loved and cared about them and believed in them and whose life example was worthy of respect.

4. *Reinforce what you want.* Individuals are shaped by the consequences of what they do.[1] You should be on the lookout for times when your children are doing what you want them to do, or are moving in that direction, and then immediately let them know you saw what they did and liked or appreciated or admired it. Focus on knowing what you want in your child and responding favorably when you see it happen. Research has consistently shown that people are more motivated by being acknowledged or otherwise rewarded for what they do right than when they are admonished for what they do wrong. Approaching it from this angle turns around the way parents often operate. Many parents spend most of their time attending to what their children do wrong: "Stop doing that." "That wasn't any good." Instead of concentrating on catching a child doing something wrong, the effective parent concentrates on catching a child doing something *right*, and then making a big deal of it.

It doesn't have to be a major success that you respond to. In the beginning, the key is to react favorably to any positive occurrence, even if it is all but obscured by a flood of negative ones. What you are looking for is any progress, any movement at all in the direction of what you want. The art in all this is to raise the threshold of your response bit by bit: reinforce actions that are just a bit beyond what the child has typically done up to now. The technical language for this is reinforcing *successive approximations* of the highest form of the behavior you want to occur.

Besides reinforcing your children, teach them to reinforce themselves. One way to keep oneself going forward in one's life is to be watchful for when we do something right and letting ourselves know it was good. Many people waste their energy denigrating themselves for their failures, and in the process wind up ignoring their successes. Then they wonder why they get discouraged and quit. Teach your children to ask themselves at the end of the game or the end of the day, "What did I do right today?" and to give themselves a pat on the back for it.

5. *Create opportunities for good things to happen.* You don't have to be passive and wait for good things to occur with your children and then respond positively to them. You can rig success, as it were. You can get your children into situations where they are more likely to move in the directions you hope they will. Some situations hold out greater possibilities than others. So, if you believe in certain kinds of activities—say, lifetime sports—arrange for your children to parti-

cipate in them, and then reinforce them for doing so. If you want your children to have a variety of sports experiences when they are young, set that up to whatever extent you can. If a particular coach or team is likely to encourage personal responsibility for skill development or whatever it is you favor, arrange that. If you believe in hiking and climbing, do it with your child.

As your children get older, you probably will be less able to determine their contexts, but you can still be active in identifying and pointing out good opportunities for them to consider. Pointing out possibilities is not the same thing as requiring children to take advantage of them. It is simply being an "advance scout" looking for new horizons for your children. It involves using your experience and insight to bear on expanding your children's perception of the range of available alternatives.

6. *Push your child.* I know the idea of pushing children has a bad connotation, and indeed if taken to an extreme it can have very negative consequences.[2] Nevertheless, good parents and teachers and coaches do push children, and the intensity of the push increases as the children get older. They push wisely, in directions that will truly benefit the child, and they aren't harsh and overbearing about it. But they do apply a steady, persistent pressure on their children to move in particular directions. Children develop and learn by confronting nonthreatening—or at least relatively nonthreatening—challenges and pressures to take themselves a bit beyond where they are now. Adults who motivate children communicate an insistence that the children confront these challenges. It is a gentle, caring, and respectful insistence, but there is seriousness about it, a no-nonsense quality. People—parents, siblings, coaches, teachers—who push in the best sense of the word hold up a high standard of engagement with life to children and push them to match up to that standard.

There you have it, the six principles of parent impact: Clarify your priorities and commitments regarding your children. Be an example of what you value. Share your convictions and hopes (and musts) with your children. Focus on reinforcing what you want rather than criticizing what you don't want. Create opportunities for children to develop in the ways you favor. Finally, wisely and gently but persistently push them in the direction you want them to go.

The challenge is to integrate and employ all the principles concurrently. It is a matter of being watchful moment by moment for the chance to use one or the other of the six principles, and to do so in your own natural way and in a manner appropriate to your child and the particular situation. There is no precise formula or technique to use in every situation. The effective use of these principles depends on your sensitivity and judgment.

YOUR CHILD'S PARTICIPATION IN SPORTS

The preteen years are a time for a child's playful involvement with sports. The emphasis ought to be on social occasions, being with family and friends, physical activity as an end in itself, and having fun. There ought to be spontaneity and joy mixed in with any necessary organization and order. The accent ought to be on the positive. Parents should be on the lookout for a child's effort and accomplishments, and be sure to acknowledge and praise them. The early years are crucial years, because so often this is when children become caught up with a sport and become self-motivated in it. If there is no fun and success for the children when they first get a taste of a sport, many times their involvement stops right there.

Should parents encourage young children to participate in organized sports? My answer is yes—with the attitude that childhood is a time for trying a lot of things, and sports is among the promising possibilities. This is in contrast to communicating to your child that sports is a requirement of childhood. Invite your child to get involved in sports, and if the child's answer is no, that is acceptable. However, it leaves open the possibility that in the future the invitation will be repeated.

If you recall, Ken Heise's question was: Do you force children to participate, absolutely insist that they involve themselves in sports? In my view, you don't. A child's integrity must be respected; it has a higher priority than a sports experience. A parent can tell her child in some detail how getting into sports could have good outcomes, but then the choice must be the child's. If the child chooses to participate in sports, however—and particularly as the child gets older and more deeply involved—I think parents have the right to expect the child to be responsible about it and to do it right.

When your child is young, the focus ought to be on exposure to a variety of sports possibilities. We need to remember that sports includes more than the major spectator sports, and I have listed a number of the many sports possibilities elsewhere. Be careful not to let gender, class, and racial stereotypes unduly limit your sense of what is possible for your child.

Although in general it is good to give children a taste of the wide range of possibilities sport has to offer, we must recognize that there are some children who lock in very early to a particular sport. They know what they want to do and just want the time and opportunity to do it. Variety isn't what they want and very likely isn't what they need. Gary Kasparov, the great chess player (another sport possibility, by the way), knew at a very early age that he wanted to concentrate his energies on chess. Kasparov's parents were both avid chess players, so it was a natural part of life in his home growing up. They didn't insist that Gary get into chess, and in fact had some concern that he was becoming too immersed in the game. They recognized his remarkable talent and deep interest in chess, however, and gave him all the support they could. He became a great chess champion and by all accounts a well-adjusted adult.

It is important not to get locked into the view that sports involvement for your child has to be in conflict with some other activity—say with giving his or her all in school. Sports and school can both be top priorities and complement one another. A parent doesn't have to say, "Remember, school comes first over sports." Instead, tell your child: "Give both school and sports 100 percent! Don't play off one activity against the other. Use your commitment and excellence in one to set the standard for and guide your involvement in the other."

A child's early years are a time to learn the most basic skills of a sport. If children pick up bad habits when they are young, these habits can be very difficult, and sometimes impossible, to break later on. If you can, get your child good coaching in the fundamentals, for example the straight overhand throw in baseball or the correct hand action when shooting a basketball. Even if you aren't an expert in some sport, you can take part in teaching some of its fundamental skills to your child yourself. Most often they aren't all that complicated. Go to a bookstore and find a book on teaching rudimentary skills of most popular sports. Teaching a sport's fundamentals to your child can be a rewarding, shared experience for you and your child. As children grow older they will need expert coaching, but early on you can be very helpful.

After age 11 or so, children's connection to organized sports becomes widely differentiated. Some, if they haven't already done so, decide sports is not for them and do other things. Those who continue to participate in sports span the spectrum from those who regard it as a relatively insignificant activity to those who make it the organizing principle of their lives. What ties together all youngsters involved in sports, however, and makes them more alike than different is that they are all teenagers going through what teenagers go through. That means, for one thing, that to some degree you can count on all adolescents to look upon sports as a social occasion. Even for the most highly motivated and ambitious athletes, sports is a time to be on a team and with their friends, and it is a chance to meet new people. How well this social side of sports goes will be a concern to them. You can count on the relationship with the coach being on their minds. You can assume that it matters to them whether or not sports provides them with some fun and excitement. You can be very sure that they see sports as a place to be competent and effective, stack up well against others, set themselves off as separate and distinct individuals, and win others' respect as well as their own respect for themselves.

As a parent, you can acknowledge and validate your children's concerns by showing that you understand and share them and want to provide support or guidance. Putting your child's concerns into words, defining them, and bringing them out in the open helps your child recognize that you understand and relate to his or her reality. This gives the child the feeling that he or she is not alone with the concerns, and that is empowering. Also, doing this makes the child's concerns more explicit and allows the child to focus on them and manage them more effectively. The goal is to communicate, "I know what it is like to be you." You might say something like, "I'm picking up that something is worrying you about your relationship with your coach. Is that right? I'd like to hear how that's going for you."

As children get older you can begin to direct their attention to the triad of athletic motivations and actions I described in Chapter 8: self-expression, learning and development, and contributing to others and the team. Thus, your exchanges with your children can center on queries such as (in your own words, of course): Are you playing *your* game? Are you revealing your uniqueness and strengths as a player? Are you learning and growing as a player? Are you discovering things about yourself and other players and your sport? Are you supporting other players on the team? Are other players and the team better because of your presence?

It is especially important to promote a purposeful and thoughtful approach to sports. Instead of setting sports goals for your child or critiquing the technical aspects of sports performance, work on getting the child to do that for him- or herself. Use questions such as: What are your goals in track this year? Do you have a strategy for improving your one-hundred-meter time? What did you learn from the last meet that you can use to improve your performance next time? Do you want my help in setting up some goals and figuring out ways to accomplish them?

What you hope is that your child will develop an analytical approach to sports participation, as well as the ability to monitor his or her own performance and to adjust goals and strategies in light of what he or she observes. With the help of coaches, many athletes review videotapes of themselves. Perhaps you could help out by videotaping your child. It wouldn't have to be much: a time or two at bat in baseball, a couple of practice jump shots or free throws. Then sit with your child and ask: What do you see? What was good? What can you improve? I don't think you have to provide expert analysis and advice yourself. The point is to get your child in the habit of assessing and modifying his or her own athletic performance.

A useful skill to teach your child is how to ask others for help. I have observed that invariably successful people in every field know how to ask for help. Successful athletes at the highest levels have a clear idea of what they are trying to achieve and where they need to improve, or they know that they aren't clear about those things and need to be. Guided by that self-understanding, they seek out a coach and ask for help, and then listen carefully to the advice they receive and employ it to elevate their level of performance.

In all the years I played organized athletics—from the peewee leagues when I was nine through the Babe Ruth league and American Legion and high school and Army ball and in college and the amateur leagues—never, not once, did I approach a coach and ask for help. More than that, I never thought coaches owed it to me to reach out and offer to help me. As I saw it, coaches were my judges, not my helpers. Coaches were there to decide what position I played, whether I started, and how much time I got in the game. That was it. I tried to pick up what I could from watching other players or listening to what they said to me in passing. I don't remember ever directly asking another athlete how he did things or asking him to look me over and make some recommendations. This was part of a pattern for me. I operated the same way at home, in school, and everywhere else.

I have reflected on why I approached things in the way I did during those years. As I think about it, I never was really expected to do anything else. It strikes me how much of my childhood was a matter of showing up somewhere and someone else taking it from there. As much as anything, my job in life until I was out of high school was basically to show up. I showed up for school. I showed up for sports practice. I showed up at the scheduled time for the television program or movie. I showed up for dinner. I showed up at Palace playground and every once in a while at St. Clair playground in the evenings and on weekends. I bring this up because I see a lot of kids now behaving in sports, in school, and in life as I did then. They show up and react and cope or get bounced from here to there like balls on a pool table, or they lay low to stay out of danger.

You can begin encouraging children to ask for help when they are quite young. Say to your child, "When you need help from me, I want you to ask for it, okay?" and then keep repeating that message. You and your child might sit down and work through how he or she could approach a coach for help, and then talk about how it went afterward.

There are many ways to do this, and you can learn what works for you by trial and error.

Something else you can do as a parent is be a keeper of the big picture. When your child becomes caught up in the immediate problems and concerns of sports, you can place it in its larger context. On a daily basis a sports activity can be captivating and all-consuming. Without trivializing your child's experience, you can be the one to raise questions that the child may be distracted from raising. You can be the one who brings up the effect this sports involvement is having on the kind of person the child is becoming. You can be the one to bring up issues of character and education and the future. You can be the one to ask how happy this sports experience is making the child. You can be the one who reminds your child that there are alternatives to this sports situation, that the child doesn't have to be doing this, and that playing this sport or being on this team is a choice the child is making, a choice that can be changed.

You can also be a reality check. I have sketched out some ideas about what accounts for success in sports in Chapter 8. Those are the kinds of things you may want to interject into your conversations if your child seems to be unaware of them or ignoring them.

Whether you will get a chance to talk about any of this with your children depends on your relationship with them. If your children are readers, perhaps you can give or suggest books, including biographies, novels, and self-help books, that highlight or illustrate points you wish to make or issues you want to raise. Probably what is most important is not what you say but rather what you represent to your children. You can try model these attributes in your own life. Children can pick that up. You don't always have to be direct.

PROMOTING SPORTS EXCELLENCE

In Chapter 8 I described a study that examined how individuals who have reached the highest levels of accomplishment in various fields developed their capabilities so fully. As well as top athletes, the study included musicians, mathematicians, scientists, and physicians. In this section I will describe the findings regarding the practices employed by parents of the children who later became top athletes.[3] After outlining what these parents did, I will broaden the discussion to a consideration of two social and cultural factors—the popular culture and schools—and their influence on achievement among children. As a parent, you function within the larger cultural context, and you must fully take that into account.

The athletes examined in the study were Olympic swimmers and world-class tennis players: elite athletes in what might be termed middle-class sports. I believe that the study's findings have wide generalizability, however. I note great similarity between the approach of these parents and that adopted by the parents of the future mathematicians, scientists, physicians, and artists. What the parents of these superior athletes did with their children may well have been good parenting, *period*.

The investigators found that the parents of the future athletic champions were deeply concerned about their children and willing to do the best for them at all stages of their development. In their earliest years, the children learned of their parents' personal commitment to them and their welfare. As one parent put it, "I would have been happy if Jean had been good at other things [besides athletics]—and just to try to do something really well. Whatever it required of us, we would have been happy to do." And one of the athletes said about his mother, "She was just there to support me in anything I did."[4] The researchers concluded that the willingness of parents—and often, siblings—to give encouragement and support was a significant distinction between the families of these top athletes and other families. It was the basis upon which the importance of success and the method of achieving it—diligent hard work—became powerful personal guidelines for the children.

Usually at least one parent had a definite interest in athletics and competition and encouraged the child to participate in sports activities at an early age. The parents with the sports interest had rationales for advocating sports for their children. Some saw sports as a way to keep the child busy and working toward a goal. Some viewed arcticulate sports as an opportunity to make new friends and be part of a team. Some saw a link between physical fitness and positive thinking. Some saw a tie between competitive sports and character and personal integrity. Some thought sports competition would bring out the best in their children, give them worthwhile goals, and teach them the value of hard work, discipline, and organization. None of these parents encouraged their children in sports to produce great athletes. Instead, they saw athletics simply as a healthy activity for their children. Remember what earlier chapters in this book concluded about what sports does and doesn't do in the areas these parents considered important.

The introduction of these children to sports was natural and informal. For the child, sports was something the family or friends were doing, and the child took part in it. Sports was one activity among many; there wasn't a big to-do about it. Perhaps a parent would give a tennis racquet as a gift to the child and the child would hit balls against a wall while the parent played a match, and then the parent would join the child for five or ten minutes. There might be some informal lessons in the process. The sports activity was brief and low-keyed, and stressed rudimentary skills and having fun.

During the early years, before organized competition, these parents communicated certain values to their children. The parents stressed achievement, success, doing one's best, and using one's time constructively. Over and over, they emphasized excelling, working hard, and not wasting time. This was not just in relation to sports: these values also held for school or playing the piano, for example. As one parent said, "We always told them that there were right and wrong things and we always stressed that anything worth doing is worth doing well. No matter how many times you do something, you always try to do it as well or better than the time before." An athlete said, "We were pretty much a highly disciplined family approaching jobs with the idea, 'Do the best you can or don't do it at all. Do it until it is done well.'"[5] Some parents pointedly reminded their children when they strayed from these values. In other cases, the parents' influence was more indirect. One athlete said, "I guess my father never really said directly to me that 'I want you to become good at whatever you do.' But there must have been some sort of influence."[6]

One pattern the researchers noted was that the children were expected to share in household chores and responsibilities and to do them well. Another was that the parents modeled the values they were attempting to impart to their children. These parents were hard workers themselves and did their best in whatever they attempted. One athlete described something he observed in his father: "It can't just be good enough to pass. I can remember my dad working around the house—if something wasn't right, he'd rip it up and redo it."[7] These parents' lives demonstrated to their children that being responsible and disciplined paid off.

These parents stressed self-sufficiency in their children. They did not breed dependency. They wanted their children to be independent people, free of others' control, including the control of peers and the parents themselves. The parents' message to their children was, "You go ahead and make your own decisions. Do what you want to do, and we'll support you. And if anything goes wrong, we'll be there to help you."

When the child grew older and entered the teen years and became involved in organized sports, these parents continued to be attentive and encouraging and willing to help. They were spectators who followed their children's exploits in sports closely and cheered them on. But they also looked for ways they could be more actively helpful. For instance, these parents helped with transportation. They monitored the child's progress closely and always knew when things were going well or poorly. They encouraged good practice habits. They helped their children in setting up training and practice schedules, and encouraged their children to stick with the regimen and gave them approval when they did. They assisted their children in getting special help when they needed it. They pushed their children to work hard and make use of the resources available to them to improve.

These parents shared an attitude toward losing: although it wasn't as good as winning, losing was acceptable if the child had done his or her best and saw the defeat as an incentive to work harder and do better next time. Over time, as the child grew older, there was a continuation, and to some extent an escalation, of the measured support of sports that the parents had offered all along: "It's your choice whether to participate in sports or not, and there are many other good things to do. Have a good time, but along with that, if this is something you choose to do, take it seriously and give it your best. Don't waste your time or the coaches' time. We'll back you all the way."

This is what these parents did, and their children became fine athletes. As far as I can tell, sports gave these children personal satisfaction; they felt good about their participation in sports. Moreover, these young people both respected their parents and stayed close to them—which is important to note at a time when so many children are alienated from their parents and even disdainful of them. We can never be sure exactly how much the actions of these parents accounted for the success in sports their children attained. Many factors go into making a superior athlete. But everything I know suggests that what these parents did—and that includes the kinds of people they were, the example they set for their children—made a significant and positive contribution to producing the quality athletes these children became.

THE CULTURAL CONTEXT

Recall from the last chapter the terms that were used to describe superior athletes: "Independent." "Strong emotional commitment." "Great desire." "Determined." "A fighter." "Excellent competitor." "Stays out there and does whatever has to be done." "Practices twice as hard as anyone else." "Doesn't give up." "Can get down and come back." I speculate this is what achievers are like in any area of life. Bring these qualities to any endeavor and the odds are greatly increased that you will attain success in it. To the degree that the parents of these excellent athletes advanced their children's acquisition of these traits, they deserve great credit. In particular they deserve credit because they were operating amid forces counteracting what they were trying to do with their children.

There is ambivalence in our culture about the characteristics achievers possess, and about achievement itself. On the one hand, as a culture we applaud and reward high achievers in sports and every other walk of life—business, politics, the arts, entertainment, and the rest. We admire their intelligence, skill, determination, and concentration. We admire their accomplishments. On the other hand, as much as we admire these people, sometimes they make us uncomfortable and disapproving. There is a widely held view that achievers are excessive, pushy, elitist, selfish, even undemocratic. Who do they think they are to be so intense, so driven, so ambitious, so connected to what they are doing, so focused on themselves, so consumed by trying to get somewhere? Who are they to strive like this, to compete like this? And who are the parents who promote this kind of behavior in their children?

High-achieving children and the parents who want their children to be high achievers in sports or anything else are not getting a clear, unequivocal mandate from the rest of us. I will illustrate this point by discussing two aspects of the culture close to the lives of young people: the popular media and schools.

The Popular Media

The popular media—television, radio, films, music, wide-circulation magazines, video games—are a remarkably pervasive influence in the lives of practically all children. You cannot really understand the lives of children unless you understand the extent of the impact of mass media and investigate how it works. The mass media are so ubiquitous that it is fair to say that they are raising this country's children at the same time as their parents are. The medium of television has set up shop in your living room, and in all likelihood it occupies more of your children's time and attention than you do.

Not only are the media raising children at the same time as parents are, they are educating them at the same time as the schools are. Just as the schools do, the media teach children what is true and important and preferable and right, and, if research is to be believed, the media fill up more hours of potential instruction time than the schools have available to them. The next time you watch a television show with your children (a kids' show, a situation comedy, a soap opera, an adventure show, a sports event, the news, anything) or listen to one of your children's CDs, or read one of the magazines your children read, or see one of the films they go to, or look on as your child plays a video game, ask yourself, "If this were a school, what would be today's lesson about how to conduct one's life?"

I believe there is one big lesson that comes through to children from the media—one that results from many individual lessons. That big lesson is a particular set of basic beliefs and values. Basic beliefs and values are what distinguish a culture, and the culture that the media teaches very powerfully to children is the *consumer culture*. This consumer culture conflicts and competes with what the parents of the successful athletes described above were trying to accomplish with their children. For the purposes of comparison, I will call what these parents were trying to impart to their children the *achievement culture*.

In this book I have described the goals of childhood in terms of the resolution of issues of mastery and identity and the development of character and self-esteem. The consumer culture has a much simpler and in many ways more appealing message. Its message is that *happiness* is the top priority in life. Happiness in this framework is equated with states of good feeling, the most prominent among them being pleasure, enjoyment, fun, excitement, titillation, and immediate interest. Simply put, the consumer culture tells children that the point of life is to do what it takes to feel good. Everything else is secondary to that, mostly just a lot of smoke adults blow at you.

How do young people come by those good feelings according to the consumer culture? By consuming things: taking them in, having them, owning them. And of course there is a great way to consume right at hand: attending to the media and buying its products—the sneakers, the fast food, the games, the clothes, and all the rest. Those are sure-fire ways to get the positive emotional charge—interesting, exciting, fun experiences—you are looking for.

What is especially appealing is that the child doesn't have to prepare, doesn't have to think about anything, doesn't have to work up a sweat, or be anything in particular to get what he or she wants. You can feel good right now by doing nothing more than watching the show or paying your money for the movie or concert or buying the Big Mac. It is as easy as that.

You don't have to worry about anything either. It is all safe. There is nothing scary about it. There is no risk to you. You aren't putting yourself on the line. You are not going to get hurt. This is a very attractive and enticing message to children, who can feel very vulnerable.

The media is always watchful for opportunities to connect to any desires that youngsters have that the media can satisfy, or claim to satisfy. Good examples are children's yearnings for power, status, and attractiveness in the eyes of others. The media takes advantage of these desires: validates and glamorizes them and links itself and the products it sells to attaining them. What children learn is that any want they experience is just fine. They don't have to ponder whether what they want is good for them and others, or if there is something else they ought to go after instead. In fact, children learn that they don't have to figure out what they are doing or why they are doing it. The idea they pick up is that if it itches, scratch it—consume.

The media can both jump on and create a bandwagon. Notice how cleverly it plays on and contributes to children's desire to be "with it," on top of the action, up on the latest. The media has always promoted the value of being on the cutting edge, and it has always held itself in its various manifestations as the way to get there. Of course there are considerations such as whether the latest is necessarily the best or most appropriate or most rewarding, but who needs to get into all that? How does that sell a CD?

The parents of the successful athletes in the study described above might not use the term "achiever culture," but that is what they represent and foster in their children, and it is what helps produce good athletes. The ideals and ways of the achiever culture run counter to those of the consumer culture. For one thing, the perspective on happiness is fundamentally different in the achiever culture. Rather than viewing happiness as a state of *emotion*—that is to say, good feelings—the achiever culture regards happiness more as a state of *mind*. It is the *conclusion* you reach about yourself that you are living a life you can be truly proud of. The feelings that accompany the conclusion—among them gratification, contentment, and sense of worth—are rich and enduring.

Thus, happiness within the achiever orientation is an outgrowth of a decision you reach about yourself; it is not a transitory feeling. And you have to earn the decision you come to about yourself, you can't select it or buy it. You earn it by the way you live. You may try very hard to tell yourself and others that you are proud of how you are living, but if your actions don't warrant that characterization, in your quiet moments the truth will come through to you. As hard as you try to divert your attention from what you are really doing with your life—through amusements, through drugs, through rationalizations and denial—the truth will come through to you and you will have to live with it, and that doesn't feel good at all. You can't kid yourself forever.

The achiever culture is not hostile to pleasure and consumption. However, it stresses creativity and productivity over watching and consuming. It differentiates lasting satisfaction—a pervasive sense of well-being and harmony with oneself—from pleasure, which is fleeting and less fulfilling. The achiever culture says to children that marshaling their resources, testing their limits and then going beyond them, and contributing to others are the best vehicles to long-term satisfying experiences and a satisfying life.

Unlike the media, the achiever culture says to a child that the future matters and that he or she needs to prepare for it, which includes doing things now that won't produce results until later. With the media, only the present matters: do it now in order to get the payoff now.

The achiever culture asserts that living a good life is not always safe. It involves taking risks, putting yourself on the line, and facing the danger of failure and dealing with it when it happens, as it most certainly will in a life lived to the fullest. In the long run, it won't do to spend your life watching others take chances and glorying in or identifying with their victories and defeats. Life is a game you have to play yourself if you want to make a positive difference in the world and be truly happy.

The media and the commercial world it represents have a myriad of products to sell, and they depend on consumers sampling from as many of them as possible. With that being the case, it follows that they are going to promote the values of variety and diversification. Alternatively, the achiever culture says to pick your spots, specialize, do what really matters to you. Slow down, dig in, quit dabbling. Get good at something. Do something worthwhile. Attend to your own life. After all, that is what the stars are doing. While you give them your time and energy and money, they don't know you are alive.

Historically, the popular culture has set youth against parents by denigrating parents or making them seem irrelevant. Musical performers and standup comics are among those who do this very effectively and very profitably. In effect they say to young people: "You are cool, and I'm even cooler. We are in this together in opposition to 'them' [parents, teachers, the clergy, police, and all but a few politicians], who are out of touch and trying to run your life." Usually the message is that even though parents might be nice and mean well, they don't really matter. At the same time parents are trying to maintain a family identity, stay close to their children, and provide guidance to them, there are voices in society telling children, "You're one of us."

Even though the media predominantly sells the concept of instant happiness through consumption, it does send a mixed message. It is mixed principally because the achiever culture is often the content of the media that children consume. The media frequently portrays successful people, heroic people, exceptional people making good things happen. In sports, children get to watch the finest individual athletes and championship teams perform and witness examples of remarkable struggle and accomplishment. This is what attracts the attention of an audience.

Even though the message from the media is somewhat mixed, the generalization still holds: the more wrapped up children are with the media, the stronger the dose of the consumer culture they are going to get. You can contribute enormously to your child's athletic success—and overall success in life—if you counteract that by transmitting the achiever culture to your child.

Schools

As for schools (and here mostly I am thinking of public schools), they sincerely want children to achieve academically and they attempt to reward scholastic excellence. At the same time, however, most schools are made a bit uneasy by the qualities possessed by high-achieving individuals—intensely focused, highly determined, emotionally committed, and so on. Typically, it is too extreme, driven, and somehow unsettling in the school culture. This is not to say that the achiever traits are totally disparaged in schools. Rather, it is that the emphasis tends to be directed elsewhere: for example, toward values and personal qualities that contribute to collective efforts in the classroom and to a climate of mutual caring and support. There is certainly nothing wrong with those values and personal qualities, or schools' attempts to foster them. The question is whether these qualities are stressed at the expense of, or to the detriment of, other worthwhile values and qualities such as passion, dedication, concentration, and diligence, traits that go into producing sports success as well as exceptionality in other areas of life.

Listen to school professionals and you'll hear them casting individuality, independence, and competition in a negative light. Schools tend to see individuality in opposition to community, independence in opposition to interdependence, and competition in opposition to cooperation, with the latter in each pairing being the favored value. The problem is that high achievers are very often highly individualistic, independent, and competitive people. The oppositions that the schools establish are not as dichotomous as they fear. People can be both very individualistic and very supportive of community, both independent and interdependent, and both competitive and cooperative. The best athletes, for instance, are highly competitive against the opposition or a rival for a position on the team and at the same time highly cooperative with the coach and other players.

Tolerance is another highly cherished value in schools, but often this translates into being nonjudgmental and accepting of others and oneself. Achievers are not known for being relativistic, however. To them, some values and some actions are better than others, and they make that known. Schools are often put off by and attempt to tone down what they see as the intolerance of achievers, the way they rigorously judge others and themselves. The issue is whether in doing so the schools round off the edges, so to speak, of achievers and render them less vital people, including in sports.

Schools characteristically view self-importance negatively, as a lack of proper humility and concern for others. But the fact of the matter is achievers are very self-important. They are motivated by a sense of their importance as distinct and unique human beings. It matters greatly what they do and how well they do it because they matter greatly to themselves. Self-importance is not necessarily antithetical to recognizing others' importance and showing concern for them. In fact, seeing high importance in yourself can help you to see it in others and to act accordingly. Often people who don't think they are important themselves project that feeling onto others and treat them as if they don't count for much either. Also, achievers in sports and elsewhere are prideful people. They are proud of what they are doing and becoming, and they use this pride to inspire themselves to stay on course. They have too much pride in themselves to slough off or quit or back down when things get rough. However, schools may view this pride coupled with self-importance as arrogance and presumptuousness and try to bring it down a peg or two.

Public schools reflect the larger society in which they function. Over the past thirty years, with the emergence of various group movements, the social discourse has tended to emphasize personal and social equality, and schools have picked up on this. As praiseworthy as equality is as a concern and an ideal, it also must be kept in mind that individual expression and achievement ultimately involve qualitative distinctions. There is a real tension between a press for equality and individuals' quest for true excellence. Schools have tended to downplay this tension, but it has to be acknowledged.

Whatever else public schools may want to do or feel pressured to do, they must first find a way to get their students through the system without a hassle, and this is a captive population that includes many who would just as soon not participate in the system and many who can barely survive in the system even when they try. In addition (and where might they have learned this?) large numbers of students operate from the premise that unless teachers can manage to make school interesting and fun, why bother? Finally, there are students who see school as a hoop to jump through, which they are willing to do as long as it is kept low to the ground. In light of this reality, administrators and teachers may talk about maximums, but everyone knows they will be happy with minimums. The schools' actual message to students usually goes something like this: "Don't miss too many classes. Do what you are told. Complete most of the assignments (we'll try to make them interesting and fun). Don't make trouble. Go along with the group. Do that, and you'll be fine. We'll approve of you, pass you, and give you a diploma. If you want to do more than that, that would be good, we'd like that, but it is up to you; you really don't have to succeed here."

After-school sports is often the one place in children's school life that holds out the clear, unequivocal expectation that they push themselves to the limit and stand out from others, and it is often the only place that provides the opportunity and support they need to do just that. To the extent that this is the case, sports can serve usefully as a model to the rest of the school of another way of doing business.

If you aren't in position to ensure that your child is in a school that truly promotes individual excellence, here again, as in the case of the popular culture, you have the challenge to transmit some other ideals and ways to your child in order to contribute to their achievement in sports and other areas.

I do worry that as a culture generally we are losing sight of the fact that people are most themselves and happiest when they are creating and producing, not consuming or having things done for them. I think of the farmer in the field from dawn to dusk; the man or woman working six and seven days a week starting a business; the basketball player working on her jump shot hour after hour. The challenge for parents is to help their children prepare to confront the challenges of life, which, I believe, in addition to loving and being loved and becoming a decent human being, includes doing productive, needed work that reflects one's humanity and singularity. One of the greatest problems of our time is that people, no matter what their age, can't find any work to do that evokes their passion and commitment and makes them feel as if they count for something. For so many youngsters, life is a matter of existing in an world where there is much to do and much to buy but where nothing really matters all that much, including themselves.

If you want your child to live with honor and ardor and dedication and efficacy, in athletics and elsewhere, to use a sports metaphor, the ball is in your court. I don't mean to place too much pressure on you as a parent, but if you don't do it I don't know that anyone or anything else will. You may hear that you really aren't the vital force in your children's lives, especially as they get older, and that something else is—the media, school, peers, the government. People will tell you to ease off, lay back, go along with the program. But *you* are the program, so much more than anything or anybody else is. Mothers and fathers and families are the key to what their children become. That is what I have learned from a career of working with children, and that is why I primarily address this book to parents rather than the professionals who serve them. I have concluded that you as a parent are society's best hope and that everything rides on what you do with your children.

IN CLOSING

Thank you very much, Ken, for taking the time to write. I hope this answer to your letter has been helpful to you. Writing this book has been good work for me. I have grown over these months. I feel much clearer about myself and sports and parenting and the larger issues of our lives and where things go for me from here. It has been very rewarding to have said all this for the first time. If it hadn't been for you, I wouldn't have had this experience, and I am grateful to you for it. All my best to you and your family.

And thank you also to the person reading this, for taking the time to consider the thoughts I have about sports and children's lives. I have been very aware of your presence from first word to last. I hope this book has put sports in a clearer perspective and stimulated your thinking. I hope I have given you direction and that you feel now at the end that this book has been worthy of your time.

Notes

CHAPTER 1

1. For a discussion of some of my conclusions, see Robert Griffin, *Underachievers in Secondary School* (Hillsdale, NJ: Lawrence Erlbaum Associates, 1988), pp. 79–98.

2. The article Ken read: Robert Griffin, "Helping Athletes Excel in the Classroom—And on the Field,"*Clearing House*, vol. 65, no. 1, September–October 1991, pp. 23–25. It was reprinted in slightly modified form and with a new title: "Helping Athletes Excel in Sports and in School," *Education Digest*, vol. 57, no. 6, February 1992, pp. 69–73.

3. If you wish to review my perspective on education, the best source is Robert Griffin, *Teaching in a Secondary School* (Hillsdale, NJ: Lawrence Erlbaum Associates, 1993).

4. Kenneth Petress, "Let's Return Athletics to the Curriculum," *Education*, vol. 113, no. 1, Fall 1992, p. 64.

5. Dale Brubaker and Gerald Austin, "Sport's Unsung Heroes: Creative Leadership and the Silent Curriculum," *Education*, vol. 113, no. 1, Fall 1992, pp. 102–103.

6. Eric Margenau, *Sports Without Pressure* (New York: Gardner Press, 1990).

7. Ibid., p. 1.

8. Ibid., pp. 11–12.

9. Ibid., pp. 9, 20.

10. Ibid., p. 1.

11. Ibid., p. 20.

12. Judy Oppenheimer, *Dreams of Glory: A Mother's Season with Her Son's Football Team* (New York: Summit Books, 1991).

13. Ibid., p. 12.

14. Ibid., p. 15.

15. Ibid., p. 17.

16. Ibid., p. 324.

17. Penelope Eckert, *Jocks and Burnouts: Social Categories and Identity in the High School* (New York: Teachers College Press, 1989).

18. For a description of these social categories, see Robert V. Bullough Jr., J. Gary Knowles, and Nedra A. Crow, *Emerging as a Teacher* (New York: Routledge, 1992), pp. 170–174.

19. James Michener, *Sports in America* (New York: Random House, 1976).

CHAPTER 2

1. The material in the following paragraphs was informed particularly by Leslie Williams and Doris Fromberg, *Encyclopedia of Early Childhood Education* (New York: Garland, 1992), pp. 214–219, 229–234, 238–240, 259–263. Also, refer to the books by David Elkind. A classic of its kind is Elkind, *All Grown Up and No Place to Go* (Reading, MA: Addison-Wesley, 1984).

2. Judy Oppenheimer, *Dreams of Glory: A Mother's Season with Her Son's Football Team* (New York: Summit Books, 1991), pp. 12, 160.

3. Here I lean on the theories of the late psychologist Erik Erickson, which stress the importance of mastery. See a discussion of Erickson in relation to sports in Stephen Figler and Gail Whitaker, *Sport and Play in American Life*, 2nd Ed. (Dubuque, IA: Wm. C. Brown, 1991), pp.126–127.

4. If you want to explore intellectual development further, look into the theories of the late Swiss psychologist Jean Piaget. A place to start: Ray Fuller, *Seven Pioneers of Psychology: Behaviour and Mind* (New York: Routledge, 1995).

5. The best theorist in this area in my view is Nathaniel Branden. See his book, *Six Pillars of Self-Esteem* (New York: Bantam/Doubleday, 1993).

6. D. Stanley Eitzen and George Sage, *Sociology of North American Sport* 5th ed. (Madison, WI: Brown and Benchmark, 1993) pp. 109, 110.

7. C. Roger Rees, Frank Howell, and Andrew Miracle, "Do Sports Build Character?" *Social Science Journal*, vol. 27, no. 3, July 1990, p. 304.

8. Andrew Miracle and C. Roger Rees have co-authored a book that explores character development in sports: *Lessons of the Lockeroom: The Myth of School Sports* (Amherst, NY: Prometheus Books, 1994).

9. A good source on social development is Stephanie Hanrahan and Cindy Gallois, "Social Interactions," in Robert Singer, Milledge Murphy, and L. Keith Tennant, editors, *Handbook of Research on Sport Psychology* (New York: Macmillan, 1993), pp. 623–646, especially pp. 625–629.

10. Jay Coakley, *Sport and Society*, 4th ed. (St. Louis: Times Mirror/Mosby College Publishing, 1990), p. 337.

11. Ibid.

12. Glyn Roberts, "Motivation in Sport: Understanding and Enhancing the Motivation and Achievement of Children," in Singer, Murphy, and Tennant, *Handbook of Research on Sport Psychology*, p. 412; Coakley, *Sport and*

Society, p. 337.

13. Educator Theodore Sizer writes well on the importance of self-respect. See his book, *Horace's Compromise: The Dilemma of the High School* (Boston: Houghton Mifflin, 1992), p. 59.

14. A fine book that explores self-respect is Charles Murray, *In Pursuit of Happiness and Good Government* (New York: Simon & Schuster, 1988).

15. Erik Erickson also wrote about adolescent identity. See his classic book, *Identity: Youth in Crisis* (New York: Norton, 1968).

16. Hanrahan and Gallois, "Social Interactions," p. 625.

17. For example, see Joan Lipsitz, *Successful Schools for Young Adolescents* (New Brunswick, NJ: Transaction Books, 1984), p. 10.

18. For reference to this research, see Robert Brustad, "Youth in Sport: Psychological Considerations," in Singer, Murphy, and Tennant, *Handbook of Research on Sport Psychology*, p. 698. See also, Sam Chambers, "Factors Affecting Elementary School Students' Participation in Sports," *Elementary School Journal*, vol. 91, no. 5, 1991, p. 413.

19. For a discussion of how mental pictures motivate us, see William Glasser, *Take Effective Control of Your Life*, (New York: Harper & Row, 1984).

20. Richard deCharmes coined this distinction. Read about him in Eric Johnson's excellent book, *Raising Children to Achieve: A Guide to Motivational Success in School and in Life* (New York: Walker, 1984), pp. 8–9.

21. A book that makes this point is Penelope Leach, *Children First: What Our Society Must Do—And Is Not Doing—For Our Children Today* (New York: Alfred A. Knopf, 1994).

CHAPTER 3

1. Jay Coakley, "Socialization and Sport," in Robert Singer, Milledge Murphey, and L. Keith Tennant, *Handbook of Research on Sport Psychology* (New York: Macmillan, 1993), p. 578.

2. Coakley, "Socialization and Sport," p. 578. See also, Jay Coakley, *Sport and Society*, 4th ed. (St. Louis: Times Mirror/Mosby College Publishing, 1990), pp. 324–327.

3. Quoted in Coakley, *Sport and Society*, p. 325.

4. Herbert Marsh, "The Effects of Participation in Sport during the Last Two Years of High School," *Sociology of Sport Journal*, vol. 10, 1993, pp. 18–43.

5. Sam Chambers, "Factors Affecting Elementary School Students' Participation in Sports," *Elementary School Journal*, vol. 91, no. 5, May 1991, p. 418.

6. Jay Coakley, *Sport and Society*, pp. 322–336.

7. A theorist who has written about these processes is Eugene Gendlin. See his book, *Focusing* (New York: Bantam Books, 1981).

8. Richard Morin, "True Jocks, with Brawn and Brains," *Burlington (VT) Free Press*, September 21, 1993, p. 8A.

9. As reported in *USA Today*, July 11, 1997, p. 140.

CHAPTER 4

1. Lee Schreiber, *The Parent's Guide to Kids' Sports* (Boston: Little, Brown, 1990), pp. 9–10. This is a fine resource for parents on the subject we are considering in this book. Check with libraries and bookstores for availability.

2. If you want to explore moral development theory, a good place to start is the writings of the late Lawrence Kohlberg. For example, Lawrence Kohlberg, "Moral Stages and Moralization: The Cognitive-Developmental Approach," in T. Lickona, editor, *Moral Development and Behavior: Theory, Research, and Social Issues* (New York: Holt, Rinehart, and Winston, 1976), pp. 31–53.

3. For example, see a summary of Norma Haan's theory of moral development in Brenda Bredemeier and David Shields, "Moral Psychology in the Context of Sport," in Robert N. Singer, Milledge Murphey, and L. Keith Tennant, *Handbook of Research on Sport Psychology* (New York: Macmillan, 1993), pp. 591–592. If you want to go into the background of this, read Carol Gilligan's seminal book, *In a Different Voice* (Cambridge, MA: Harvard University Press, 1982).

4. Bredemeier and Shields, "Moral Psychology," p. 578. The entire Bredemeier and Shields chapter on morality and sport (pp. 587–599) in Singer, Murphey, and Tennant is a good introduction to this topic.

5. Bredemeier and Shields, "Moral Psychology," p. 595.

6. Ibid., p. 596.

7. See Jay Coakley, *Sport and Society*, 4th ed. (St. Louis: Times Mirror /Mosby, 1990), p. 79; Jay Coakley, "Socialization and Sport," in Singer, Murphey, and Tennant, *Handbook of Research on Sport Psychology*, p. 580.

8. Ibid., p. 576.

9. Ibid., p. 580.

10. Ibid., p. 579.

11. Ibid., p. 579.

12. Judy Oppenheimer, *Dreams of Glory: A Mother's Season with Her Son's Football Team* (New York: Summit Books, 1991), p. 327.

13. Ibid., p. 324.

14. Coakley, *Sport and Society*, p. 79.

15. Ibid., p. 80.

16. C. Roger Rees, Frank Howell, and Andrew Miracle, "Do High School Sports Build Character?" *Social Science Journal*, vol. 27, no. 3, July 1990, p. 313.

CHAPTER 5

1. Jay Coakley, *Sport and Society*, 4th ed. (St. Louis: Times Mirror/Mosby,

1990), p. 323.

2. See Thomas Sowell, *Inside American Education: The Decline, the Deception, the Dogmas* (New York: Free Press, 1993), pp. 24, 26.

3. For the meaning high school sports can have for a town, see H. G. Bissinger, *Friday Night Lights: A Town, a Team, and a Dream* (New York: Harper/Collins, 1991).

4. See D. Stanley Eitzen and George Sage, *Sociology of North American Sport, 5th ed.* (Madison, WI: Brown and Benchmark, 1993), p. 105.

CHAPTER 6

1. Jay Coakley, *Sport and Society*, 4th ed. (St. Louis: Times Mirror/Mosby, 1990), p. 56. Also, a book that discusses sports and women's place in society is Mariah Burton Nelson, *The Stronger Women Get, the More Men Love Football: Sexism and the American Culture of Sports* (New York: Harcourt Brace, 1994). Another is Susan Cahn, *Coming on Strong: Gender and Sexuality in Twentieth-Century Women's Sports* (New York: Free Press/Macmillan, 1994).

2. For a review of this research, see Sam Chambers, "Factors Affecting Elementary School Students' Participation in Sports," *Elementary School Journal*, vol. 91, no. 5, May 1991, p. 421. See Diane Gill, "Competitiveness and Competitive Orientation in Sport," in Robert Singer, Milledge Murphy, and L. Keith Tennant, *Handbook of Research on Sport Psychology* (New York: Macmillan, 1993), pp. 321–322.

3. See Carole Oglesby and Karen Hill, "Gender and Sport," in Singer, Murphy and Tennant, *Handbook of Research on Sport Psychology*, p. 723.

4. Coakley, *Sport and Society*, pp. 181–182, 289.

5. Lyn Brown and Carol Gilligan, *Meeting at the Crossroads: Women's Psychology and Girls' Development* (Cambridge, MA: Harvard University Press, 1992).

6. D. Stanley Eitzen and George Sage, *Sociology of North American Sport,* 5th ed. (Madison, WI: Brown and Benchmark, 1993), p. 110.

7. President's Council on Physical Fitness and Sports, *Physical Activity and Sport in the Lives of Girls: Physical and Mental Health Dimensions from an Interdisciplinary Approach*, Spring 1997 [Online: http://www.coled.umn.edu /KLS/crgws/default.html].

8. Ibid.

CHAPTER 7

1. For a discussion of this phenomenon, see Stanley Eitzen and George Sage, *Sociology of North American Sport*, 5th ed. (Madison, WI: Brown and Benchmark, 1993), pp. 76–77. See also Barry McPherson, James Curtis, and John Loy, *The Social Significance of Sport* (Champaign, IL: Human Kinetics Books, 1989), pp. 178–179; and Wilbert Leonard II, *A Sociological Perspective*

of Sport, 4th ed. (New York: Macmillan, 1993), pp. 191–193.

2. As reported in Eitzen and Sage, *Sociology of North American Sport,* p. 77.

3. Ibid.

4. Ibid., p. 314.

5. John Hoberman, *Darwin's Athletes: How Sport Has Damaged Black America and Preserved the Myth of Race* (Boston: Houghton Mifflin Company, 1997), p. 9.

6. Richard Lapchick, *Five Minutes to Midnight: Race and Sports in the 1990s* (Lanham, MD: Madison Books, 1991), p. 261.

7. Ibid., p. 260.

8. Ibid., p. 261.

9. Merrill Melnick, Donald Sabo, and Beth Vanfossen, "Educational Effects of Interscholastic Participation on African-American and Hispanic Youth," *Adolescence,* vol. 27, no. 106, Summer 1992, pp. 295–309.

10. Eldon Snyder and Elmer Spreitzer, "High School Attendance Among Black, Hispanic, and White Males: A Research Note," *Youth and Society,* vol. 21, no. 3, March 1990, pp. 390–399.

11. As reported in *USA Today,* June 27, 1997, p. 10C.

12. As quoted in Hoberman, p. 8.

13. Ibid., p. 242.

CHAPTER 8

1. Benjamin Bloom, ed., *Developing Talent in Young People* (New York: Ballantine Books, 1985), p.158.

2. Ibid., p. 150.

3. Ibid., p. 176.

4. Ibid., pp. 239–240.

5. Ibid., p. 544.

6. See Craig Wrisberg, "Levels of Performance Skill," in Robert Singer, Milledge Murphey, and L. Keith Tennant, *Handbook of Research on Sport Psychology* (New York: Macmillan, 1993), p. 64.

7. Robert Sternberg, *Beyond I.Q.: A Triarchic Theory of Human Intelligence* (New York: Cambridge University Press, 1985).

8. Howard Gardner, *Frames of Mind: The Theory of Multiple Intelligences* (New York: Basic Books, 1993).

9. For a review of this research, see Joan Duda, "Goals: A Social-Cognitive Approach to the Study of Achievement Motivation in Sport," in Singer, Murphey, and Tennant, *Handbook of Research on Sport Psychology,* pp. 421–433. Duda is an important theorist in this area. For the application of these distinctions to education, see the writings of John Nicholls. For example, J. Nicholls, P. Cheung, J. Lauer, and M. Patashnick, "Individual Differences in Academic Motivation: Perceived Ability, Goals, Beliefs, and Values," *Learning*

and Individual Differences, vol. 1, 1989, pp. 63–84.

10. See Stuart Biddle, "Attribution Research and Sport Psychology," in Singer, Murphey, and Tennant, *Handbook of Research on Sport Psychology*, p. 446.

11. As reported in Glyn Roberts, "Motivation in Sport: Understanding and Enhancing the Motivation and Achievement of Children," in Singer, Murphey, and Tennant, *Handbook of Research on Sport Psychology*, pp. 413, 416; and Duda, "Goals," pp. 422, 427, 428, 429, 431, 432.

12. Biddle, "Attribution Research," p. 446; and Duda, "Goals," pp. 423, 429.

13. David Pargman, "Individual Differences: Cognitive and Perceptual Styles," in Singer, Murphey, and Tennant, *Handbook of Research on Sport Psychology*, pp. 387–388.

14. All in Singer, Murphey, and Tennant, *Handbook of Research on Sport Psychology*: Yves Vanden Auwelle, Bert de Cuyper, Veerle van Mele, and Randy Rzewnicki, "Elite Performance and Personality: From Description and Prediction to Diagnosis and Intervention," pp. 270, 274; Richard Suinn, "Imagery," p. 493; Robert Rotella and J. Dana Lerner, "Responding to Competitive Pressure," p. 532; and Robert Nideffer, "Attention Control Training," p. 545.

15. I have reviewed the sports literature to confirm my perception that successful athletes are committed to understanding what is going on, and to going forward in the most rational way possible. One confirming example comes from the remarkably thoughtful athletes George Will describes in his book, *Men at Work* (New York: Macmillan, 1990).

16. Vanden Auweele et al., "Elite Performance," p. 270.

17. Ibid., p. 274.

18. Suinn, "Imagery," p. 495.

19. Lawrence Harrison, *Who Prospers? How Cultural Values Shape Economic and Political Success* (New York: Basic Books, 1992).

20. There is much good writing in the area of achievement. The two best books on achievement in children I have encountered are Bloom, *Developing Talent in Young People*, and Eric Johnson, *Raising Children to Achieve: A Guide for Motivating Success in School and in Life* (New York: Walker, 1984). Both books may be out of print, but check with a library; it should be able to obtain copies for you.

CHAPTER 9

1. The theorist who best articulated this position is psychologist B. F. Skinner. See the book he wrote for general readers: B. F. Skinner, *Beyond Freedom and Dignity* (New York: Knopf, 1977).

2. For example, see Joan Ryan, *Little Girls in Pretty Boxes: The Making and Breaking of Elite Gymnasts and Figure Skaters* (New York: Doubleday, 1995).

3. The summary of parenting practices with young athletes was compiled from Benjamin Bloom, ed., *Developing Talent in Young People* (New York:

Ballantine Books, 1985), pp. 143–189, 215–231, 507–549. In particular refer to pp. 507–549, where the editor provides generalizations about talent development.

4. Ibid., p. 147–148.
5. Ibid., p. 146.
6. Ibid., p. 219.
7. Ibid., p. 147.

Further Reading

American Sport Education Program. *SportParent*. Champaign, IL: Human Kinetics, 1994.

Blais, Madeleine. *In These Girls, Heart is a Muscle*. New York: Warner Books, 1996.

Cahn, Susan. *Gender and Sexuality in Twentieth-Century Women's Sport*. New York: Free Press, 1994.

Coaching Association of Canada. *Straight Talk About Children and Sport: Advice for Parents, Coaches, and Teachers*. Buffalo: Mosaic Press, 1997.

Dodson, James. *Final Rounds: A Father, a Son, the Golf Journey of a Lifetime*. New York: Bantam, 1997.

Fine, Aubrey, and Michael Sachs. *The Total Sports Experience—for Kids*. South Bend, IN: Diamond Communications, 1997.

Fortansce, Vincent. *Life Lessons from Little League: A Guide to Parents and Coaches*. New York: Doubleday, 1995.

Frey, Darcy. *The Last Shot: City Streets, Basketball Dreams*. New York: Touchstone, 1994.

Gent, Peter. *The Last Magic Summer: A Season With My Son*. New York: William Morrow, 1996.

Hoberman, John. *Darwin's Athletes: How Sport Has Damaged Black America and Preserved the Myth of Race*. Boston: Houghton-Mifflin, 1997.

Kessler, Lauren. *Full Court Press: A Season in the Life of a Winning Basketball Team and the Women Who Made It Happen*. New York: Dutton, 1997.

Nelson, Mariah Burton. *The Stronger Women Get, the More Men Love Football*. New York: Harcourt Brace, 1994.

Ripken, Cal, Jr. *The Only Way I Know*. New York: Viking, 1997.

Ryan, Joan. *Little Girls in Pretty Boxes: The Making of Elite Gymnasts and Figure Skaters*. New York: Warner Books, 1996.

Teague, Grant. *Coaching in the Classroom: Teaching Self-Motivation*. Waco, TX: CORD Communications, 1994.

Wolff, Rick. *Good Sports: A Concerned Parent's Guide to Competitive Youth Sports*, 2d ed. Champaign, IL: Sagamore, 1997.

Woods, Earl. *Training a Tiger: A Father's Guide to Raising a Winner in Both Golf and Life.* New York: HarperCollins, 1997.

Index

About the Author

ROBERT S. GRIFFIN is Professor in the College of Education and Social Services at the University of Vermont. His writings have been published in the *Harvard Educational Review*, *Educational Theory*, *Teachers College Record*, and *Education Digest*. He is the author of two previous books on the education of adolescents.